10.95
-5

METAPHORIC PROCESS

METAPHORIC PROCESS

The Creation of Scientific and Religious Understanding

By
Mary Gerhart, Professor of Religious Studies
and
Allan Melvin Russell, Professor of Physics

Hobart and William Smith Colleges
Geneva, New York

WITH A FOREWORD BY PAUL RICOEUR

TEXAS CHRISTIAN UNIVERSITY PRESS • FORT WORTH

Library of Congress Cataloging in Publication Data
Gerhart, Mary.
    Metaphoric process.

    Bibliography: p.
    Includes index.
    1. Religion and science—1946–   2. Knowl-
edge, Theory of.   3. Metaphor.   I. Russell, Allan
Melvin. II. Title
BL240.2.G47   1984   261.5'5   83-15614
ISBN 0-912646-82-9
ISBN 0-912646-86-1 (pbk)

Designed by Whitehead & Whitehead

Table of Contents

PART 2: NEW UNDERSTANDINGS THROUGH METAPHOR

Foreword

THIS WORK by Mary Gerhart and Allan Melvin Russell is a fine example of interdisciplinary collaboration, begun in the classroom and completed in a book written in common. In this way, the voice of the physicist and that of the theologian are at once distinct and complementary.

The book's originality lies in the initial decision not to look for the key to the relation between science and religion in a new refinement of the theory of language—thereby running the risk of losing out on the resources of an easy eclecticism that an "ecumenical" theory of language might have provided—but instead to knock, as the authors say, on the door of *experience*. This decision led them ineluctably into the troubled waters of ontology.

The book proceeds step-by-step, from the most formal resemblances that establish a simple parallel between forms of knowledge to the convergence of diverse perspectives on the being of the world and on being in the world which give rise to a genuine interconnection of science and religion, on the edge of mystery.

The first area of confrontation concerns *theoretical mediations* which, on both sides, make of experience, whether "external" or "internal," something more than direct and immediate observation. The exploration of these theoretical mediations leads to the critical examination of the classical oppositions between objective description and subjective feeling. Science and religion present instead comparable "methods" in the manner in which what is considered to be experience is mediated by each person. One can thus draw parallels between comparable processes of growth and critical examination, of permanence and decline.

Knowing in process becomes in this way the motto common to the scientific "method" and to the religious "method."

In its constructive part, the book takes a decisive step: after having developed the notion of "field of meaning" (Gerald Holton's *themata*), the authors give a central role to metaphor in the *change* these fields of meaning undergo. The strategic role attributed to metaphor constitutes the most remarkable contribution of this work, to the extent that metaphor, far from being limited to a linguistic artifact, is characterized by its epistemological function of discovering new meanings. What is at stake is still knowing in process but considered in its "nascent moment." In this sense metaphor is a thought process before being a language process. It is indeed to the theoretical mediations of experience that metaphor makes a powerful contribution, at the point where observation is joined to theory.

Having arrived at this point, the authors do not try to evade the difficulties surrounding the question of the *referent* of metaphor in the two areas concerned: an ontology seems necessarily implied by the epistemology. And the claim is made in theology just as it is in physics: to consider, with David Tracy, "Jesus as the Supreme Fiction" (in homage to Wallace Stevens) is to say what the "object" of religion *is like*, by opening up new possible worlds and new possibilities of being in these worlds.

In moving from epistemology to ontology, the problematic also moves from parallels to convergence and even to fusion. The authors indeed venture to designate the intending of the entirely-other as the common intending of the two experiences carried to the furthest point of expression. This common intending makes natural philosophy and theology, the developed forms of physical experience and of religious experience, refer to the same world. It is also against the backdrop of this common intending that one can make the assertion that science and theology "need" one another and mutually serve to mediate one another.

I strongly recommend this book, as much for its audacity as for its intellectual honesty. Here we have a professor of physics and a professor of religious studies who have dared to venture beyond the safe shores of language and to push an epistemological inquiry beyond itself and into the very heart of ontology. But they earn the right to this audacity by the frankness of their questions, the didactic force of their remarkably well chosen examples, and the rigor of the advance of a meditation leading from the parallel between science and religion to their exchange. This book thus reveals itself to be an excellent illustration of its central theme: knowledge in process.

Paul Ricoeur

Preface

THIS IS A BIDISCIPLINARY WORK. That is, it was written by two persons from different academic points of view, a professor of religious studies and a professor of physics, both convinced that human enquiry has a common philosophical foundation. Together, as a kind of duet, we construct an argument to show that religion and science are not only compatible but cooperative and complementary fields of intellectual endeavor. The task, we believe, could not have been done by either of us working alone, because literature in the two fields is not sufficient for the work. What must be combined are the experiences of having studied, in some depth, what is known separately in each of the two disciplines, experiences not ordinarily part of the background of any one scholar.

We want to thank the faculty and students from still other disciplines, not only at our own institution but also at SUNY Stony Brook, Niagara University, and The University of Edinburgh, who have listened to our insistences with a critical understanding and have made comments and suggestions that have influenced our work. Finally, we wish to acknowledge the many others who contributed to the production of the manuscript.

We want to applaud our colleges, Hobart and William Smith, for their appreciation of this kind of bidisciplinary work and their willingness to bear the expense of having two professors working in the same classroom with a small group of students. The idea that the liberal arts are more than just a collection of courses from different disciplines rarely is expressed in such expensive curricular terms.

Finally we wish to alert readers to our heuristic intent—this is not a book to get lost in. Our ambition is that when our readers

have finished hearing what we have to say, they will have gained
an enlarged appreciation for the varieties of ways of knowing—
not merely a naive pluralism but a depth of understanding that
can recognize knowledge-in-process as the dynamics of thought
in humans determined to know their world.

Mary Gerhart
Allan Melvin Russell
October, 1983

METAPHORIC PROCESS

PART 1

CONVENTIONAL UNDERSTANDINGS IN SCIENCE AND RELIGION

CHAPTER ONE

Introduction to Part 1

For those who hold that language is the data of philosophy, religion and science appear to say what they say in the same ways. And the things which are claimed may or may not be believed. While this state of affairs may be an improvement over the requirement that truth be indubitable, it fosters a naive intellectual pluralism. Only by returning to the grounds of epistemic claims can we find science and religion compatible, even cooperative, activities directed toward coming to know and to understand.

THE TURN TOWARD LANGUAGE

"The world," said Ludwig Wittgenstein, "is the totality of facts, not of things."[1] With this opening in the *Tractatus* (1921), ontology was moved from speculative philosophy to the level of discourse, and linguistics became the dominant philosophical form. In particular, with respect to the philosophy of science, the effect of this shift was to replace in the mid-twentieth-century concern for the objects of science with a new emphasis on the claims of science. How convenient for the philosophers of religion who from the beginning had to take account of the linguistic aspect of theological objects and claims. The possibility of resolving the disputes between science and religion, disputes that had gone on for centuries, seemed within reach.

One of the first philosophers to apply Wittgenstein's ideas to the conceptual foundations of science was Norwood Russell Hanson in his celebrated *Patterns of Discovery* (1958). Hanson's dictum that all seeing is necessarily "seeing as" or "seeing that" effectively replaced the operationalism of the nineteenth century with a quasi-linguistic context in which an object must be embedded before it can be seen.[2] The older operationalism, in which a physical quantity was understood in terms of the operations required for its measurement, came to be understood as a form of ostension. Hanson argued that a theoretical framework, a "context" is needed before anything can be seen as something. It is not sufficient merely to point.

Four years later, in 1962, Thomas S. Kuhn published his influential essay on "The Structure of Scientific Revolutions."[3] In it he argued that the progress of the history of science has not been one of steady data accretion and theory development. Rather, advances have been made in conjunction with radical shifts in the way some aspects of science are considered. In the nineteenth century, for example, enormous success was achieved by describing electric and magnetic phenomena in terms of a continuum of fields. But modern physics and chemistry could not develop until the dominant view of the world changed from the continuum of fields to the discreteness of atoms, a change which led eventually to the concept of light quanta and quantum mechanics.

According to Kuhn, such shifts of "paradigm" bring about crises in science, crises which are not resolved until "revolutions" are seen historically. In effect, Kuhn's thesis served to introduce a political metaphor into the history of science, thereby giving science an aspect of fashion in much the same way that political parties are or are not in vogue. Certain modes of thinking are then understood to be *au courant* in science as they are in social affairs.

For better or for worse, these three emphases—on the linguistic nature of things, on the role of context in interpretation, and on the political model for scientific change—all contributed to a shift in the mid-twentieth-century understanding of science. Science has now become widely thought to be not the way one understands the world but merely one possible interpretation of a certain aspect of collective human experience, something now akin to the late twentieth-century understanding of religion. During the same period a retreat from doctrine into uncritical ecumenism became prevalent in religious understanding: one interpretation of the sacred is as good as another.[4]

LINGUISTIC-ORIENTED RESPONSES

The result has been that many authors, both theologians and scientists, rushed to explain how a psychosociolinguistic understanding of science makes the latter entirely compatible with religion. Their approaches ranged from the linguistic/literary on the one hand, stressing aspects of science which can be seen as mythical and mysterious, to the linguistic/analytical on the other, focusing on those aspects of science which can be identified as metaphoric and nominative.

In his book, *Religion and the Scientific Future* (1970), for example, Langdon Gilkey explored the uses of myth in what he took to be a scientific culture. He argued that myths referring to sacred origins, myths which were a backward look to "an essential cosmic order in which man's freedom must participate," have been replaced by two contemporary myths which are a forward look to "a potential existence in the open historical future which man's freedom may create." These two myths are the liberal view of cosmic and historical progress (evolution) and the Marxist view of historical dialectic. Both, according to Gilkey, are a variation on the modern gnostic myth of autonomy. Both represent "the dominant source of confidence, reassurance, and meaning in the present West: the myth of the new scientific man." In this context, Gilkey saw the task of religion as one of overcoming the gnosis of the myths. Religion restores the paradox inherent in the mystery of human destiny and freedom: without the aid of "multivalent, symbolic language" essential to religious myth, secular myth resides in the self-contradiction of attempting to control, however creatively, the human subject whose essential characteristic is that of freedom. Religion also reminds the "scientific elite" that it is their fellow citizens and not objects that they propose to control and that, as Gilkey wrote, "there is a good deal less freedom in the scientific knower and controller than most descriptions of the potential uses of science in the future seem to assume." In his epilogue, Gilkey studied the relation between myth, philosophy, and theology. He argued for the necessity of myth in both science and religion and for theological and philosophical reflection necessary to understand how it is that "the future comes to be out of the present."[5]

Harold Schilling, working from the side of scientist, documented what he saw as the emergence of *The New Consciousness in Science and Religion* (1973). The focal point of his work is most succinctly stated in the appendix, "On the Meanings of 'Mystery,'" first published in *The Iliff Review* 1972. There he discussed certain common usages of mystery, such as "that which arouses curiosity," "the still-to-be-explained," "forbidden secrets," and "superstition" as pseudo-mystery. Schilling replaced these common understandings with what he called authentic understandings of mystery—"the quality of the unknown," "the quality of the known," and "the radically questionable." He traced this new concept of mystery through contemporary science and Biblical religion and saw it as the distinctive feature of the "new consciousness." Schilling had an essentially progressive view of science. He looked forward to the next scientific revolution, named it the "galactic" reformation, and said that it would displace the Einsteinian universe as the latter did Newtonian physics. Schilling skillfully plied the notion of "depth" to show how no single scientific theory can be of itself conclusive: within each discovery are embedded multiple other discoveries, each potentially destructive of the seeming truth of the former: "It seems clear, then, that it is no longer legitimate to equate any level that happens to be the lowest (most interior) one known at any given time with the hoped-for ground level of matter."[6] He then reiterated alternative understandings of Biblical religion, showing how they complement scientific (or humanistic) faith and in what sense both science and religion capitulate in the face of evil. Schilling attempted to defend religion against the falsification disputes but in the end had to resort to hope for a blessed future as an ultimate response.

Two books published in the later 1970's indicate in their titles their intention of contributing to the linguistic parsing of religious and scientific issues. Ian Barbour's *Myths, Models and Paradigms* (1974) disavows the functional differentiation of science and religion wherein the "function of scientific language is the prediction and control of nature and that of religious language is the expression of self-commitment, ethical dedication, and existential life-orientation." Indeed, Barbour cautioned that "the price of this division of labour is that religion would have to give up any claims to truth, at least with respect to any facts external to one's own commitment."[7] Earl MacCormac, in his *Metaphor and Myth in Science and Religion* (1976) shared Barbour's conviction.[8] The strategy of both, however, was to refine the linguistic approach, again finding instances of myths, models, paradigms, and metaphors in both science and religion. Barbour, for example, studied the diverse functions of language, with emphasis on the cognitive function of religious language. In his treatment of the role of models, he contrasted the interpretation of observations in science and the interpretation of experience in religion, asserting that the latter is less theory-laden than the former. On the role of conflicting paradigms, he saw a resolution in the discovery of "overlapping observation-statements."

There is a common aspect to all these works—they examine science and the processes of science as literary and religious genres and find, in so doing, that scientific language is not significantly different from other language, scientific paradigms no different from other myths. They see, in short, no conflict, no problem. In this view, science seems to have abandoned its absolute claims and become a discipline which, like so many others, operates under the aegis of language, requiring only an interpretive context and subject to revolutions of fashion. In addition to *De Gustibus non Disputandum est,* we now have *De Scientiis Naturalibus non Disputandum est.* It would almost seem that we are allowed to choose the science we want to believe as we can choose the music we like to hear.

Kuhn, Hanson, and even Wittgenstein would not hold such unprincipled relativism as valid. However, it is sometimes useful to express the most extreme view in order to sense the potential scope of the situation. To express the contemporary state of affairs in the philosophy of science somewhat less extremely, one might say that there is hardly any claim of fact that a scientist can make today that cannot be challenged by some person on some valid grounds. How like this situation was the situation in which theologians found themselves a century ago!

WHAT HAS GONE WRONG?

This can hardly be the resolution Alfred North Whitehead called for in the Lowell Lectures of 1925 when he gave such forceful expression to the reasons we should be concerned with the interrelationships between science and religion. "We have here the two strongest general forces . . . which influence human beings and they seem to be set one against the other—the force of our religious institutions, and the force of our impulse to accurate observation and logical deduction. . . . When we consider what religion is for humanity and what science is, it is no exaggeration to say that the future course of history depends upon the decision of this generation as to the relations between them."[9]

In the nineteenth century, when broad achievements in science led enlightened intellectuals to challenge religious dogma, it was thought that religion would have to undergo radical change if it was to exist in collaboration with science. Religion would have to become more "scientific" if you will, for, after all, was not science the only road to true knowledge?

The battle was to be waged on the classic philosophical field of the true and the false. But that field was found to be a quicksand bog in which no discipline could get a footing. Wittgenstein may have turned things into facts but, after careful subsequent analysis, the facts could not be distinguished from fiction. And herein lies the success of the linguistic approach.

That success seems to have been achieved by rendering science as less than scientific, by claiming in implication that science expresses its knowledge in the same way that religion does. We are left with forms of story-telling in science which are not self-evident forms of understanding. The same could be said for religion.

The linguistic approach fails, in part, because of its tendency to substitute forms (abstractions) for structure, and elements (myths, metaphors) for patterns or relations. Science is thereby reduced to a collection of aspects. It is ironic that reductionism, a term used pejoratively to describe some scientific methodologies, should now be applicable to techniques used to describe science itself. Reductionism fails here as elsewhere because it loses the important awareness of the way that the whole is greater than the sum of the parts.

The linguistic approach fails in another way. It overemphasizes the role of story in scientific and religious explanation. A story can be an effective and valuable explanation of the world quite apart from any consideration of its relation to fact or fiction, to truth or falsity. A good story stands on its validity, on its form and structure, on how it says what it says more than why it says it. However, to understand both religion and science as only story is to obviate the grounds, the human experiences, that provide the warrants for the claims and propositions that comprise the story.

Finally, the linguistic approach fails because it cannot account for the form and structure of theory. Theory has become anathema to linguistic analysis perhaps because of a failure, after decades of effort, to substantiate a theory of linguistic development. Modern linguistics, despite the efforts of Chomsky and his followers, cannot account for the origins of language. Language, then, becomes a given. But science is not a given; religion is not a given. Both of these aspects of human life bear a theoretical relationship to human experience.

Which is not to say that we have not benefited from the movement that Wittgenstein sparked when he said that the world is a world of facts rather than things. Nor is it to say that human thought and understanding are not closely related to human language which they must certainly be. But to say that our understandings of science and religion are sufficient now that the controversy has died is to do little more than to rest content with the sense that science too has its myths while all the time the work in the scientific laboratories goes on unaffected by any such sense of resolution.

What is left? If it is indeed true that science is as badly off as it once thought religion to be, is there any possibility of progress? Is commiseration all that remains? We think not. The time has come, we believe, to explore these questions from a different point of view, to play out the game on a different field, if you will. We think that issues of the true and the false have prematurely been allowed to becloud issues of process, that an understanding of what is true must presuppose an understanding of the process of understanding itself. Ontology must be postponed in order that epistemology, what we call "knowledge-in-process," may preside. We must reintroduce and emphasize the roles that experience and theory play in the development of human knowledge. But what are these roles? First, consider the idea of theory.

TESTING FOR THEORY

Suppose that an extraterrestrial intelligence were to visit the earth for a brief period. How would it be possible for such an intelligence to see that an oak and a pine are both trees? How would it be possible for the intelligence to understand the relations between acorn and oak or cone and pine? How then could it relate acorn and cone? All of these—the oak, the pine, the acorn, and the cone—are vastly different in appearance and in the way they feel and smell. So how then are we able to relate these different things? We can relate them because we understand what they are. We understand because we have a theory of trees, and the existence of theory makes understanding possible. Theory is always *a priori* in fact even though it is always *a posteriori* in our understanding: we see things the way they are because of our theories; we know our theories, as well as their roles in our seeing, in acts of reflective understanding.

But is one theory just as good as another? Is one understanding as satisfactory as another? If the fruits of an understanding are its claims, can we say that we will accept one claim as readily as another? Surely not. Even the most radical relativist would balk at this point. Theories and their understandings give rise to claims that must be verified by experience.

THE NEED FOR JUSTIFICATION

It was a white chicken, a more or less ordinary looking chicken, that came running out of the coop. "The sky is falling in. I must go and tell the king." It is a story heard over and over again in our modern world. Only now we hear it in terms of resources, or pollution, or nuclear energy. What is our response to these exhortative cries? Only one is in keeping with two thousand years of intellectual development, and that is: "How do you know? What warrant do you have for what you claim to be the case?" Here is modern skepticism. The question that must be asked over and over again: "Tell me not what it is that you know. Tell me first how it is that you can claim to know it."

"And so you say that the sky is falling in. Tell me how you know that is so? Was it something that hit you on the head? Do you know what that might be? Did anyone see you get hit on the head?" And so it goes. We want to know why it is that Chicken Little cries out. It must be so with every claim.

It is no different with an act of faith. To say that you believe is to say that you know. "I know that my redeemer liveth." "I know that the moon is held in its orbit by the gravitational attraction of the earth." It is not the claims that call our attention. We ask, instead, for the warrants to those claims.

Our modern interpersonal sensitivity may prevent us from the challenge of faith. Courtesy may keep us from the engagement, but the challenge stands there nonetheless. One cannot believe what one wants without further question. That question stands even if one is not challenged. What grounds are there for believing in God? Is there a serious alternative to the belief that all life, including that of humans, derived from a common ancestor by mutation and natural selection?

Whatever the question, whatever the claim, the response must be that justification is to be found in and through an examination of human experience. Without experience there can be no theory and no understanding. And without experience there can be no verification and justification.

The place to begin a study of the relationship between science and religion is found, then, not in the book of language but at the door of experience.

CHAPTER TWO

Experience

THE IDEA OF EXPERIENCE, and its relationship to what we claim to know and to how we come to know it is a fundamental question in both science and religion. In this chapter we attempt to dispel the naïve notion that science bases its understanding entirely on direct experiences with an external reality whereas religion derives its understandings entirely from experiences of an "internal" kind.

DIRECT EXPERIENCE AND MATURE SCIENCE

Norwood Russell Hanson, in the first chapter of his book, *Patterns of Discovery*, described what he believed to be going on when Tycho Brahe and Johannes Kepler stood together on a hill and watched the dawn.[1] He raised the question of whether these two seventeenth-century astronomers, one who held that the sun circles the earth and the other who claimed that the earth circles the sun, saw the same thing. "Seeing," said Hanson, "is an experience."[2] Then the question becomes whether these two men experienced the same thing. Hanson concluded that they did not; we will argue that they do. Before considering this situation further, we must examine the role of experience in science in a number of other instances which are designed to make the general relationship clearer and which will afford an alternative to Hanson's formulation and conclusion. So, for the time being, we will leave these two ancient astronomers staring eastward from their dewy knoll while we look elsewhere.

Experience is certainly one of the most important components of human learning and, depending on how we choose to define experience, it may be the *sine qua non* of cognitive development. Nonetheless we wish to examine the proposition that a mature science does not advance on the basis of a scientist's direct experience with the world. In particular, modern physical science develops, at least in part, on the basis of observations that can hardly be called observations at all. They are more likely to be the quantitative output of a computer than to be numbers derived from a visual examination of some phenomenon.

In order for us to proceed, we will need a rather detailed description of a particular scientific investigation, one with information sufficient to allow us to examine the role of the scientist in enough depth to bring out the details of the scientist's experiences. We have chosen, as our example, a paleomagnetic study in which one of the authors participated. The choice was made not only because of our detailed knowledge of this work but also because it serves as an example of the research activities going on in many disciplines such as genetics or astronomy.

Paleomagnetic Geochronology

Glacial lakes deposit sediments on their bottoms as a continuous rain of fine particles, some of which are magnetic. As the magnetic particles fall through the water, they line up like little compass needles in the direction of the earth's magnetic field. They reach the bottom and subsequently become imbedded with the fine nonmagnetic particles as part of the muddy clay that builds up on the bottom of the lake. This process goes on for thousands of years. Meanwhile the earth's magnetic field is changing in intensity and direction as changes take place in the core of the planet. The implanted magnetic particles, however, are now not free to change their directions as they are effectively held in place by a matrix of clay particles which forms the bulk of the lake mud.

The orientation of the earth's magnetic field several thousand years ago is an historical scientific question of the kind thought not very long ago to be impossible of answering through "observation." We now know, however, that we have a magnetic record of that very datum. The lake mud contains a record of the direction of the ancient magnetic field in the orientation of those microscopic needles trapped on the bottom.

To measure the orientation of the magnetic particles we set off from the shore of Seneca Lake in a research vessel and, with specially designed underwater sound scanners, located a section of the lake bottom that was flat, where we could expect the muds had not been mechanically disturbed by events such as slides or slumping. A coring device was then lowered to the floor of the lake, some one hundred meters below the surface, and a mud core six meters long was extracted by driving a pipe into the bottom. The resulting core was about four centimeters in diameter and contained within it mud that was put in place over the period of perhaps twelve thousand years, all in fine layers like a roll of Necco wafers.

We then had a long tube filled with mud in which the magnetic particles were pointing in the directions they did when they were put in place thousands of years ago. How could we determine just what those directions are? The particles themselves are microscopic. When we examined them under a microscope they seemed to have no particular shape or arrangement. The only possible way to determine their orientation was to measure the magnetic field that they themselves created.

The strength and character of a very small magnetic field can be measured through the electronic detection of the changes that such a field makes in a specially fabricated magnetic material. Part of the difficulty in making such measurements arises from the requirement of making them in the presence of the strong magnetic field of the earth. Not only is the earth's field tens of thousands of times stronger than the field due to the particles themselves, but the earth's field also changes with time in a more or less random manner. This latter behavior is referred to as noise. Measuring a very small steady field in the presence of a strong fluctuating one requires a high level of instrumental sophistication. We spun our sample containing the microscopic particles, causing them to rotate at a uniform rate of five rotations per second. We then examined the behavior of our magnetic field detector—no, wait, that was said improperly; we did nothing of the kind. We connected our magnetic field detector to a computer in such a way as to cause the computer to record only those magnetic fields—no, that is not right either. The computer recorded only those electronic signals that came from the detector and varied at the rate of five rotations per second. The computer counted until a sufficient number of rotations had been completed. It then stopped the measurement process, computed the magnitude and direction of the spinning field, and instructed a teletypewriter to print the appropriate numbers onto a paper sheet and simultaneously to punch holes in paper tape corresponding to the microscopic magnetic field determined at that one point along the mud core.

The detector then moved a few millimeters down the core and the process was repeated. After three hundred to five hundred such measurements had been made along the length of the core, the scientist removed the punched paper tape and took it to another larger computer which read the tape and stored its message in computer memory. The scientist then sat down at the console of the computer, typed in the appropriate identification codes, and the screen—much like a television screen—displayed the curve that showed how the magnetic field changed direction along the length of the core. The comparison of two or more such cores of lake sediments makes possible the judgment that a certain part of one core was put in place on the lake bottom at the same time as a particular part of another core. In this way, the ancient topography of the sediments can be determined.

While geophysicists may or may not agree about the significance of such paleomagnetic observations, we may have significant disagreements about the experience of the geophysicists making the observations.

In what sense can we say that the scientists "experienced" the variation of the earth's magnetic field over the past twelve thousand years? The word "experience" certainly seems wrong in this context. Let us try again. In what sense did the scientist experience the record of the earth's ancient magnetic field? Can an examination of the punched paper tape be called an experience of the magnetic field record? We might get by with this in casual usage but it does not seem to be sufficiently accurate for our analysis. What precisely did the geophysicist at the end of the process, sitting at that computer console, experience?

Experienced was the presentation of a display, a figure drawn in light, that showed graphically just how the direction of the magnetic field changed from point to point down the core. Can we say that the changing magnetic field was experienced? Probably not. Considering the long chain of instrumental connections that were constructed between the core sample itself and the display on the screen, it would be difficult to argue in favor of the claim that the scientist "experienced" that changing field.

The situation is similar to that which one finds in high energy particle physics where an array of bubble tracks in a photograph, such as those sketched in Fig. 2.1, is studied by a physicist in an effort to gain some understanding of the interaction between high energy submicroscopic particles that could never themselves be seen. Such particles last for only a fraction of a billionth of a second after they have been generated in a collision by an accelerator beam. Does the physicist "experience" the particle production? We would say "no."

Fig. 2.1 A drawing of tracks in a bubble chamber made by the particles generated in a high-energy accelerator.

Consider now a scientific observation as it might have taken place in a biology laboratory prior to 1950. The investigator is examining fruit flies that are the offspring of irradiated parents.

The scientist looks at the flies through a low-power microscope and uses a needle to separate those with white eyes from those with red, counting carefully the number of each kind. Can we say, in this case, that the scientist is experiencing the genetic result of the mating of irradiated fruit flies? In this case we think that we can, and to do so makes it possible to distinguish the data of instrumentation, which are not directly experiential, from the data of experience itself. We do not mean to imply that the data of experience need be less precise or less quantitative than the data of instrumentation. Nor do we wish to suggest that the scientist is more or less self-conscious during the course of the direct experience (immediate) or during the course of the general experience (reflective). We wish merely to emphasize that in the mature sciences what was formerly conceived as experience is now mediated by instruments to such an extent that the experience is of an instrument and not of the natural system under investigation.

Using a terminology introduced by Bernard Lonergan, we can distinguish between our experience of bodies on the one hand and things on the other[3] by saying that the former are unmediated experiences (immediate experiences) whereas the latter are mediated experiences; that is, they are governed by some theoretical, conceptual, or abstract understanding. This understanding need not be reflective or even conscious, since the mediation of the experience takes place whether or not there is conscious reflection on the question of understanding.

In order to describe the role that instrumentation plays in the mediation of experience we need to refine some of these ideas. To begin with we will distinguish "direct experience," which may be either of a body or of a thing, from "instrumentally mediated experience" which must always be experience of things.

Don Ihde, writing about the phenomenology of instrumentation, used this way of diagramming situations of the kind we are describing as direct experience:

$$\text{HUMAN} \longleftrightarrow \text{WORLD}.$$

A first-order instrumentally mediated experience such as the experiences of Polanyi's blind man with a stick might be shown as follows:[4]

(HUMAN + INSTRUMENT) $\longleftrightarrow$ WORLD.

A second-order instrumentally mediated experience, as in the example of the paleomagnetic studies, is diagrammed as follows:

HUMAN $\longleftrightarrow$ (INSTRUMENT + WORLD).

From time to time a conflict arises between the data of instrumentally mediated experience and those of direct experience. How might we encounter and then resolve such a conflict? Consider the following situation: You are at the supermarket and have just chosen two heads of cabbage which must be weighed and priced. You hand the heads to a clerk who places them one at a time on the scale. After each head is placed on the scale, the scale buzzes, clicks, and delivers to the clerk a gummed label. The latter is affixed to the plastic wrap that covers each of the cabbages. Having finished the weighing, the clerk hands the cabbages to you and you look at the labels. One says 5.7 pounds, .51 dollars; the other 3.5 pounds, .32 dollars. As you stand there with the two heads of cabbage, one in each hand, you perceive by "hefting" them, that the one marked 3.5 pounds is heavier than the one labeled 5.7 pounds. What do you do? Your experience of the comparative weights of these two cabbages is contrary to the "official" instrument determination of their weights. Which do you believe? The answer is clear. Experience has taken precedence over instrumental data and you have no doubt that the heads are marked incorrectly.

However, such is not always the case with experience. We can be mislead by the illusion of experience or the experience of illusion so that our actual experience will not finally be given precedence. We will illustrate this kind of situation by means of four well-known visual and tactile illusions.

For the first example, examine the two lines in Fig. 2.2 to determine which of the two is longer. After you have made your judgment on the basis of your experience of these lines, then measure them. Before you do that, however, reflect on whether or not you will take a measurement that differs from your judgment to be in error. (Of course you must bracket any knowledge you may have of the Müller-Lyer illusion[5] and hence of the "correct" response; that is, you must take the experience, phenomenologically, as it comes to you.)

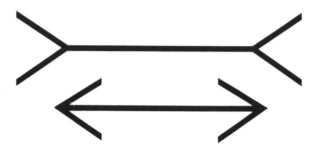

Fig. 2.2 Müller-Lyer illusion used to illustrate conflict between direct experience and instrumentally mediated experience.

For the second example, cross your index finger and your second finger (either hand) and roll a marble around on a hard surface in such a way that the marble is in contact with the ends of both fingers. Close your eyes. Do you experience two marbles? Keep trying until you do. Notice that your experience is contrary to your understanding. Even though you know there is only one marble, you still experience two!

The third example consists of dipping the first three fingers of each hand into a cup of water, each hand into a different cup. The water in each cup is at a different temperature. After a couple of minutes remove your fingers and dip them into two new cups of water. The question to be considered is which of the two new cups of water is experienced as warmer. If the new cups of water are at the same temperature, a difference in warmness will be experienced. If the left hand was initially in a warmer cup, then the left cup of the second pair will be experienced as being colder than the right.

This experiment can be carried out with several people of whom each is given different initial pairs of cups—that is, some persons are given cups with the left one warmer than the right, some given cups with the right warmer than the left, and some with the initial pair of cups containing water at the same temperature. When this group of persons all test the same second pair of cups containing water at the same temperature, some will experience the left cup as containing warmer water, some the right, and some—those whose initial cups were at the same temperature—will experience the second pair as alike in temperature. Under these conditions the members of the group will not agree; there will be no verification of their observations. They will be forced to conclude that the understanding derived from the direct experience was erroneous or at least unreliable.

Our final example consists of taking a long piece of chalk (or a short pencil), holding it firmly between the first and second fingers of one hand and then rotating the chalk about an axis that is perpendicular to the axis of the chalk and runs between the ends of the fingers. After you have done this for a number of turns the chalk will begin to feel as if it is "pinched in" at the point where it is being held. It will feel this way despite the fact that you are looking at it and know "full well" that the chalk has straight sides. Your tactile experience of the chalk leads you to an understanding that belies the understanding that is derived from your visual experience.

Now that we have demonstrated some of the kinds of difficulties that can be encountered in the understandings derived from experience, let us rejoin Tycho and Johannes as they stand on their hill in the early morning sun.

According to Hanson, these two great figures from the history of astonomy each "saw" different things. That is, their experiences were different. Just how different becomes finally apparent toward the end of Hanson's first chapter:

> Tycho sees the sun beginning its journey from horizon to horizon. He sees that from some celestial vantage point the sun . . . could be watched circling our fixed earth. Watching the sun at dawn through Tychonic spectacles would be to see it in something like this way. Kepler's visual field, however, has a different conceptual organization . . . Kep-

ler will see the horizon dipping, or turning away, from our local fixed star. This shift from sunrise to horizon-turn . . . is occasioned by differences between what Tycho and Kepler think they know.[6]

Seeing meant experiencing for Hanson, and he claimed that J. Kepler experienced the horizon "dipping or turning away." We cannot agree. No one, not even a modern practicing astronomer will, under the conditions described, experience anything but the sun making its way higher and higher into the sky.

This state of affairs becomes clearer when we realize that we do not experience the surface speed of the rotating earth (about one thousand miles per hour near the equator) nor do we experience the earth's annual rush around the sun which results in the observer's being carried in headlong flight at a rate of some sixty-seven thousand miles per hour no matter at what latitude. No one really experiences this.

The idea that scientific understandings are based on immediate experience is an error that has caused many otherwise sophisticated people to misunderstand the grounds of scientific claims. This kind of misunderstanding is nicely illustrated by Thomas S. Kuhn in his book, *The Copernican Revolution*, where he described the reaction of Jean Bodin, "one of the most advanced and creative political philosophers of the sixteenth century," to the Copernican understanding that the earth moves in an orbit around the sun. Bodin wrote:

> No one in his senses, or imbued with the slightest knowledge of physics, will ever think that the earth, heavy and unwieldy from its own weight and mass, staggers up and down around its own center and that of the sun; for at the slightest jar of the earth, we would see cities and fortresses, towns and mountains thrown down.[7]

Did Bodin react to the Copernican understanding on the basis of his own theoretical understanding? Of course not. His reaction was based on his direct experience with external objects and a common-sense understanding of the experience of stability in such objects. His mistake was his assumption that his understanding, based on a direct experience with external objects, was superior to Copernicus' understanding which was not based on direct experience.

What then is the role of experience in science? What kind of experience of the world do we have when this experience is mediated by instrumentation? A modern and sophisticated—that is to say, scientific—experience of the world is an imaginative one. The world that we know is a world of our imaginations, a world that is "made up" of our largely second-order mediated experiences. This world, this universe, is filled with stars and galaxies, with atoms and DNA molecules which we either do not experience at all (in the sense of direct experience) or which we experience in a way that so little informs our understanding (the case of a star, for example) that the experiences become almost unrelated to our understanding.

● ●

The demonstrations of the ambiguity which can accompany our sense perception of objects and Hanson's statement that "observation is theory laden" are pertinent to religious as well as to scientific experience. Two passages from William James's classic study, *The Varieties of Religious Experience* (1925), will provide us with examples.

In the following passage, James made the point that, contrary to public opinion, not all mystical experience is religious. His observation is parallel to the demonstrations of the ambiguity which can attend our sense perception of objects under scientific observation.

> . . . religious mysticism is only one half of mysticism. The other half has no accumulated traditions except those which the text-books on insanity supply. . . . In delusional insanity, paranoia, . . . we may have a *diabolical* mysticism, a sort of religious mysticism turned upside down. The same sense of ineffable importance in the smallest events, the same texts and words coming with new meanings, the same voices and visions and leadings and missions, the same controlling by extraneous powers; only this time the emotion is pessimistic: instead of consolations we have desolations; the

> meanings are dreadful; and the powers are enemies to life. It is evident that from the point of view of their psychological mechanism, the classic mysticism and these lower mysticisms spring from . . . the great subliminal or transmarginal region . . . of which so little is really known. That region contains every kind of matter: 'seraph and snake' abide there side by side. To come from thence is no infallible credential. What comes must be sifted and tested, and run the gauntlet of confrontation with the total context of experience, just like what comes from the outer world of sense.[8]

One can well imagine that almost everyone who has ever had the experience of "voices and visions and leadings and missions" has also had the conviction that these are true and also that they are religious. James cautioned that "inner" experiences (like the sense perceptions in the previous demonstrations) are ambiguous taken by themselves and that they must be "sifted and tested" in a larger context.

In a second passage, James made the point that some experience may be authentically religious, in spite of the fact that it appears to originate in a medical or psychological disorder. He dramatized the way some observers misunderstand this point when they attempt to explain away religious experience by its causes:

> Medical materialism finished up Saint Paul by calling his vision on the road to Damascus a discharging lesion of the occipital cortex, he being an epileptic. It snuffs out Saint Teresa as a hysteric, Saint Francis of Assisi as an hereditary degenerate. George Fox's discontent with the shams of his age, and his pining for spiritual veracity, it treats as a symptom of a disordered colon. Carlyle's organ-tones of misery it accounts for by a gastro-duodenal catarrh. All such mental over-tensions, it says, are, when you come to the bottom of the matter, mere affairs of diathesis (auto-intoxications most probably), due to the perverted action of various glands which physiology will yet discover.[9]

Here, Hanson's statement that "observation is theory-laden" applies in the sense that one's theory (for example, that of medical materialism) may, according to Hanson, allow one to "see" something different from the same thing "seen" in terms of another theory. In the first example, James' point was that immediate experience without any theory is indeterminate. In the second example, however, James argued that an inadequate theory involves a risk of losing the experience altogether. For example, limiting one's theory to an examination of some possible "causes" of religious experience rather than examining its fruits, luminosity, and philosophical reasonableness[10] may result in the trivialization of the experience. More importantly, the provocative thesis that direct experience does not play a role in a mature science puts us at the heart of the debate between science and religion as it has been carried on in the past. On the one hand, one might want to claim that direct experience does not play a central role in the practice of a mature science; on the other hand, one cannot deny that experience is one of the most important components of human learning and possibly the *sine qua non* of cognitive development. Initially, these two statements appear to be contradictory and to call for resolution. Are the affirmation and the denial of the necessity of human experience in science mutually exclusive, or is there some ground on which both statements, taken together, are true? It would seem that two different models of experience are needed to reconcile this apparent contradiction.

THE ROLE OF EXPERIENCE IN THE OPERATIONS OF CONSCIOUSNESS

In order to make any claims regarding the role of experience in religion and theology, it will be necessary to clarify what we mean by "experience." Experience is commonly considered to be essentially sense perception, such as stimulus-response, habit, or reflex action. We can call this model the sense-perception model of experience because it relies exclusively on the reports of the five senses. We must ask, however, if this model is adequate to our own experience of experience. Do not our recollections of most profound, rich, and meaning-filled experiences suggest that much is omitted from the sense-perception model? Where and how do our feelings, moods, and non-sensuous experiences—as discernible, for example, in an act of consciousness-raising—fit in the sense-perception model?[11] The sense-perception model excludes by definition much of what we take to be most worthwhile about our own experience.

Another model of experience can be called phenomenological. This model states that basic and prior to the reports of the five senses and undergirding all of the self's experiences is an awareness of the self as human. Technically, this "non-sensuous experience of the self" is the source of the more fundamental questions that we ask about the meaning of all our various human experiences. Three examples, each progressively lacking in anything that might be referred to as only sense perception, clarify the distinction between the sense-perception and the phenomenological models of experience.

Consider as a first example the experience of a person who has just been rescued from drowning. The sensuousness of the experience—the breathless exhaustion, the drying off and the restoration of circulation—is inadequate as a description. The renewed sense of being alive and feelings of gratitude toward those who performed the rescue cannot be explained adequately on the basis of the sensory aspects of the experience.

A second example can be found in the Christian Testament story about the disciples from Emmaus who were said to have conversed and walked some distance with the resurrected Jesus without knowing who he was. After pressing him to stay with them for supper, the scriptures say, "Their eyes were opened and they recognized him."[12] Whatever understanding one holds about the resurrected Christ, the recognition scene clearly illustrates the limitations of the sense-perception model. The text itself seems to indicate a realization that seeing is more than merely eyes being opened.

A still more pronounced example of how the non-sensuous aspect of experience surpasses the sense-perception model is a situation we have all witnessed or experienced at some time, that of reconciliation with a friend after a misunderstanding. To know that a rupture in a relationship is not terminal, to understand that mutual trust and confidence have been restored, perhaps even increased, is to experience the other and the self in a way that can be referred to only phenomenologically since it subsumes all of sense perception in its supra-sensuous intensity. Furthermore, in the relationship of the conscious to the unconscious, the phenomenological model of experience shows the inadequacy of treating the conscious as something that is merely added to the unconscious. Without consciousness, that is, without a basic awareness of the self as human, there would be no intrigue, wonder, and consternation about unconsciousness: the notion of the unconscious makes sense only when one is in a state of consciousness.

Sense perception or all that is understood to be the sensation model of experience, then, is only one part of the totality of our experience. Sense perception necessarily excludes the most basic awareness we have of ourselves: awareness of ourselves as moving, feeling, thinking, acting and deciding. In the phenomenological model, by contrast, the self as experienced is involved in a process of change and continuity, of developing and breaking relations with reality as perceived.

Certain operations of consciousness can be seen to play a central role in both science and religion. Bernard Lonergan provides us with a systematic way of understanding the operations of consciousness by differentiating among four "levels" of consciousness.[13] The first level is the observation or experience of data. Here, "observation" is the term most likely to be used by the scientist; "experience," by the theologian. The second level is the understanding of the data observed or experienced. The third level is the probable judgment about the understanding of the data observed or experienced. The fourth level is the decisive action based on the probable judgment about the understanding of the data observed or experienced. An historical event will illustrate the central but progressively transformed role of experience in the operations of consciousness as described by Lonergan.

Murders happen everyday in large cities, but on March 13, 1964, the fatal stabbing of Catherine Genovese in Queens, New York City, was reported throughout the nation and subsequently was the occasion of a moral consciousness-raising.[14] What was different about this fatal crime was the fact that thirty-eight people were aware over the period of half an hour that the woman was being stalked and attacked. They were aware of it and did nothing to help her.

The operations of consciousness can be seen in this example by applying Lonergan's analysis. Thirty-eight persons heard or watched the event. That is, they were engaged in the first operation of consciousness in that they experienced what was taking place. Even though it was around 3:00 a.m., they were sufficiently awake to know that something unusual was happening. Their *understandings* of their experience of what they heard varied: one woman said she thought it was a lover's quarrel; most others thought that someone was being attacked. The witnesses' *judgments* of their understanding of what they heard or saw were accurate: many acknowledged that they had turned on their lights (and briefly frightened off the assailant) and then turned them off again in order to see better. Most of the witnesses took *decisive action* only later, at 4:25 a.m. when an ambulance came to take the body away.

The event made national news because, whatever their understanding and judgments, none of the witnesses called the police even from the safety and anonymity of their own homes. For a few, the operation of *understanding* was faulty: for example, the woman who thought it was a lover's quarrel was content with an insufficient explanation—why should its being a lover's quarrel obstruct her understanding that it was an attack? For a few, the operation of *judgment* was faulty: they understood that someone was being attacked but refused to believe it, or they refrained from affirming what they understood lest their husbands or wives become involved. For most, the operation of *decisive action* was faulty: they were afraid; they were tired and went back to bed; they didn't know what to do.

The initial experience was progressively transformed in several ways. To understand the experience of watching or hearing the attack is both to lose some of the immediacy of the sound or the sight and to gain an intelligible grasp of what was going on. To judge (to affirm or negate one's understanding of the experience with a stated degree of conviction) is both to lose some of the fancy or fascination of identifying the assault and to gain a reasonable grasp of what is the case. To decide (to act on the basis of one's judgment of one's understanding) is both to lose the possibility of entertaining conflicting courses of action and to take a hand in the construction of one's self and one's world.

The central role of experience and its progressive transformation in the operations of consciousness are evident directly in the instance of the victim and the thirty-eight witnesses and indirectly in the instance of everyone who learned about it through the news media. That the nation was appalled and alarmed at the apathy of the witnesses indicates that the operations of consciousness are presumed to be the basis for moral responsibility.

A scientific object can also illustrate the central but progressively transformed role of experience in the operations of consciousness. Questions about the moon, for example (as abstracted from what is seen at night or imagined in the absence of observation) lead to an astronomical understanding (or explanation). The understanding of the moon is not the same as a photograph of the moon, i.e., what appears to be a luminous object in the sky. Rather the moon, itself not a source but a reflection of light, is understood as part of a celestial system. This astronomical understanding comes to be affirmed by scientists and nonscientists. Finally, the judgment or affirmation of the astronomical understanding results in the possibility of determining the phases of the moon, eclipses, tides, etc., in advance of their occurrence—the bases for decisive action by sailors and astronauts.

The idea of grace provides a parallel illustration in the field of religion. The question of grace (whether abstracted from an observed enactment or imagined in the absence of observation) leads to a theological understanding, for example that of Aquinas, where grace is understood as a kind of habit or ease in acting.[15] The understanding of grace does not exist as something tangible to the senses, yet there exist "fruits" of the presence of grace in people's lives and manifestations of the "fruits" in Western religions. Next, religious grace understood as an infused habit is affirmed to be a true understanding. Finally, the judgment or affirmation of the theological understanding is decisively communicated.

The scientist and the theologian are each engaged in the operations of consciousness every time they are aware of an object for inquiry, attempt to understand the object in terms of their respective fields of meaning, make probable judgments about those understandings of the object, and take decisive action on the basis of their judgments. We are now prepared to say that the fields of science and religion are related fundamentally in the fact that they result from the activities of human consciousness. This being so, it follows that the activities of human consciousness should be made explicit, or, at the very least, acknowledged in any claims made about the objects of inquiry in either field.

Because of the emphasis on the operations of the subject in the foregoing formulation of the relationship between science and religion, a new question arises. Is everything subjective? Is objectivity no longer possible?

Subjectivity and objectivity are among the most misunderstood terms in human discourse. Misunderstanding leads to the cliché that science is objective and religion is subjective. This cliché in turn leads to the view that science pertains to external, i.e., objectively measurable objects, and religion pertains to internal, i.e., objectively immeasurable objects. Temperature, for example, is said to be an objective reality, meaning that it is instrumentally measurable or mathematically specifiable. Religious ecstasy, on the other hand, is said to be a subjective reality, meaning that it is unique, personal, and hence immeasurable. But in addition to temperature, there are the phenomena of hot and cold to the touch to be investigated, and there may be some observable effects of ecstasy to be interpreted. Perhaps objectivity is not adequately understood by means of the concept of measurability after all.

Let us look at these two terms, "subjectivity" and "objectivity," more closely. First of all, they are designed by human beings to refer to two claims concerning human understanding: one, that the operations of a human subject are involved in any understanding; and, second, that understandings are on their way to becoming objective when they are shared by more than one person (verified) or are affirmed in terms of a particular logic (validated). Every instance of understanding (whether ultimately referred to as "subjective" or "objective") remains grounded in the situation of the self as sometimes moving, feeling, sensing, thinking, acting, or deciding. This leads us to make a minimal proposition regarding objectivity: there is no objectivity except in relation to subjectivity. Otherwise stated: there is an object only in the presence of a subject. In these terms, it makes no sense to talk about an object (a "thing") without also acknowledging a human knower. Recalling Don Ihde's diagrams for direct experience and for first- and second-order instrumentally mediated experience we notice that the arrows point both ways—to human subject and to world.

$$\text{HUMAN} \longleftrightarrow \text{WORLD}$$

The case is similar but somewhat more complex with respect to the notion of subjectivity. Subjectivity manifests itself on two levels: (1) the immediate, and (2) the mediated. Total immediacy for adults is relatively rate. Infants offer perhaps the best example of total, continuous immediacy. But even the infant as human soon begins to develop, to differentiate, and to combine capacities for more complicated operations and greater mobility. As long as speech and hearing are directed to objects which are present, however, meaning for the infant is by and large confined to a world of immediate experience.

Much of human understanding after infancy is no longer immediate, but "mediated."[16] As the infant begins to be able to handle language, words begin to refer to absent, distant, and future objects as well as to those which are immediate. Eventually the human is able to refer to things which are possible as well as factual. As Bernard Lonergan explained,

> We come to live not as the infant in a world of immediate experience, but in a far vaster world that is brought to us through the memories of other humans, through the common sense of the community, through the pages of literature, through the labors of scholars, through the investigations of scientists, through the [experience of holy men and women in religious traditions], through the mediations of philosophers and theologians.[17]

"This larger world, mediated through meaning," according to Lonergan, "does not lie within anyone's immediate experience."

It is not even the aggregate of all worlds of immediate experience. For meaning, he went on to say,

> is an act that does not merely repeat but goes beyond experiencing. What is meant, is not only experienced but also somehow understood, and, commonly, also affirmed. It is this addition of understanding and judgment that makes possible the larger world mediated by meaning, that gives it its structure and its unity, that arranges it in an orderly whole of almost endless differences partly known and familiar. . . . It is this larger world mediated by meaning that we refer to when we speak of the real world, and in it we live out our lives.[18]

Using Lonergan's analysis of mediated meaning as distinct from immediate meaning, we can now make a statement about a subject, correlating to the one made above about an object. Just as there is an object only in the presence of a subject, there is a subject only in the presence of an object. There would be no human subject unless there were at the same time the mediated meaning of some object which gives rise to an understanding of the self as experienced. A powerful example of this phenomenon occurs in the film, *The Miracle Worker*. In the climactic moment the blind and deaf child, Helen Keller, is able to mediate her experience of water with the newly understood word "water." After running from one object to another, spelling out the names of the objects on her teacher's palm, Helen points to herself to show that she understands herself to be what the word "me" means. It is not accidental that her understandings of water, earth, and stairs precede her awesome recognition of her self.

The distinction between bodies and things is important for our grasp of the concept of objectivity, and Lonergan gives us a way of clarifying the distinction. In chapter eight of *Insight*, he proposed a thought experiment.[19] He used a kitten as a heuristic device to simulate what it would be like if objectivity were not possible for human consciousness. A kitten experiences in the sense of a merely biological consciousness of an already-out-there-now-real. Although it may be attracted to a saucer of milk, for example, it has no interest in a picture of a saucer of milk once it has discovered that the picture is not capable of satisfying its basic needs. A kitten knows objects only by their relation to itself and, according to Lonergan, is capable of knowing objects only as "bodies."[20]

A human, by contrast, is capable of knowing objects not only in their relation to self but also in their relations to one another. A human can be interested in a picture of a field of flowers even though the flowers cannot be picked or smelled except in imagination. They might even look like abstract forms, attractive because of their congruence or lack of congruence or because of their relation to one another.

In other words, a human is capable of knowing objects not only as "bodies" (that is, in their immediacy, in their relation to self) but also as "things" (that is, mediately in their relations to one another). The ability to know objects as "things," theoretically and imaginatively, makes science and theology possible.

Objectivity, then, exists by virtue of the ability of humans to know objects as "things." It is not an already-out-there-now-real to be discovered, nor is it entirely an invention in the idealist sense of a purely mental act.

A good grasp of objectivity will involve a correlation of the fields of inquiry with the operations of human consciousness. "Things" are not necessarily exhaustive of what we know about some object. They are formulations which, over the years, remain because different investigators reflecting upon the object continue to affirm the understanding as expressed in the thing, the particular formulation. "Things" continue to be taken seriously because they are satisfactory responses to intelligent questions which are asked about an object. In this sense, "things" continue to be capable of assimilating the objections and counter-positions raised against them. Old "things" seldom simply die; they just fade away into new "things."

• •

The distinction between a sense-perception model of experience and a phenomenological model of experience, coupled with the explication of Bernard Lonergan's description of the structure of human consciousness, makes it possible for us to be more explicit about the difficulties with Hanson's formulation.

Hanson's central thesis is that all observation is theory-laden. In the normal application of this thesis to a sense perception requiring explicit interpretation—Hanson might use the example of a person looking at an X-ray tube—we can successfully apply Lonergan's analysis and recognize that somewhere between the levels of understanding and judgment, theory will be operative. The difficulty with Hanson's thesis, as we have pointed out, lies with what we have been calling "direct" experience and the understanding of immediate experience.

When we apply Longeran's analysis, there is no explicit judgment operative in direct experience. In the experiment with the rotated chalk that seemed to be pinched in the middle despite the fact that we knew that it was not, we can recognize operations taking place first at the level of "experience and/or observation of data." These operations would correspond to the sense perceptions. At the same time, we are presented with an understanding (the chalk is pinched). The understanding persists in the face of a denial based on other data. Now it is this understanding of an observation of the chalk—this erroneous understanding of its being pinched—that we claim is not theory-laden. To be sure some psychosensory reaction, common as far as we know to everyone, gives rise to the understanding. However, we are not willing to give this psychosensory reaction the name of theory. In this case, the reaction is understood in psychology to constitute a sensory delusion. In the absence of a satisfactory theory of illusion, experimental sciences require that instrumental data take precedence over the data of immediate experience in those circumstances where the two sources of knowledge are in disagreement.

How can we apply Lonergan's distinction between bodies and things to the case of the two astronomers watching the dawn? At the level of direct experience the sun was understood by each of them as a warm body to which they related directly and in the same way. They were both deluded into seeing the sun rise higher and higher above the horizon in much the same way we felt the chalk as pinched. However, at least one of them knew that what he was seeing was not the case, just as we did with the chalk. Thus, it is not until we reach the level of experience mediated by theory, a theory that relates the sun to the scientist not as a body but rather as a thing to other things such as the earth and the moon, that the disagreement between these two noble intellects emerges. They are now no longer operating on the level of direct experience, and they might have saved themselves the discomfort and cold of the meadow and returned to the warmth of the study where they could put pencil to paper and draw the circles (or ellipses) that more adequately represent those "things" with which they were dealing.

CHAPTER THREE

Scientific and Religious Method

THE GROWTH OF KNOWLEDGE is not an accidental or haphazard process. However, the common view of science perceives an ideal mechanism for the acquisition of knowledge, the celebrated "scientific method." At the other extreme we find a widespread notion that religious knowledge comes to us by irrational or at least non-rational means. The very notion that there is a cognitive method that leads to religious understanding comes as a surprise to many. Here we will show that the "scientific method" is not all that it is thought to be and that the "religious method" is more than is generally allowed.

SCIENCE IS NOT WHAT IT SEEMS

In the previous chapter we saw that, for a scientist, theoretical understandings prevail in spite of the contradictory nature of the naïve understanding of immediate experience. We understand that the earth hurtles around the sun at more than 66,000 miles per hour despite our naïve understanding of our experience of the earth as a huge stable surface. We understand a rug to be at the same temperature as the terrazzo floor on which it rests despite our naïve understanding, as we step off the rug with bare feet, that it is warmer than the stone floor. Hanson's contrast between what Tycho Brahe saw and what Johannes Kepler saw as they stood together on a hill watching the dawn was incorrect. The naïve understanding of our immediate experience is often not in accord with our theoretical understandings. This state of conflict can be resolved in one of three ways. We may say that the experience is paramount and that our theory is wrong, which leaves us in the state of first naïveté.[1] We may judge that our theoretical understanding is correct and that our experience is delusive, which, without further questioning, leaves us in a state of second naïveté. Or we may assert that our theory and our experience do not in fact have the same referent which constitutes a partial breakdown of our world of meanings, a situation that should not be left without further reflection or observation. Fortunately for the sake of our epistemological development the second form of resolution is the usual outcome of the conflict. That is, our theoretical understandings are given precedence over the naïve understanding of our immediate experience.

With this understanding in mind it comes as no surprise to find that a mature science derives its theoretical understandings from the data of instrumentation rather than from direct experience. At this point one might object that the scientist's perception of the data of instrumentation is experiential and that we have therefore not removed ourselves from immediate experience after all. However, the direct experience of the data is irrelevant to the development of the subsequent understanding. This is not to say that the data are irrelevant to that understanding. It is often quite the contrary. The data may be the only access we can have to the phenomenon to be understood. However, it is not the data which are being focused on here but rather the data as representative of the phenomenon. And the experience of the data as representative is a mediated experience. It is experience mediated by theoretical understanding; it is an experience of a thing and not a body.

Thus Kepler, in attempting to understand the motion of Mars, did not experience Tycho Brahe's data as numbers on a page but rather as representations of positions of the planet Mars. And once more we encounter theoretical understanding based on one or more abstractions that transcend any naïve experience of the data themselves.

So it is that a long chain of theoretical understandings, based on interpretation of instrumental data in the light of an abstraction we call an atom, results in the conception of a brick as being composed mostly of empty space. In point of fact, even an atomic scientist experiences an isolated brick as a body—a firm, hard, rigid, heavy, solid, sometimes painful object. There is no other, more sophisticated, scientific experience of a brick. We may understand a brick as a thing made up of atoms, but we experience it as a body—an apparent contradiction.

Here there is a strong parallel between scientific understanding and religious understanding. There seem to be many occasions when religious understanding prevails in the face of contrary naïve understandings of immediate experience. These prevailing religious understandings are based not on any naïve understanding of immediate experience but rather on a long chain of theological understandings based in turn often on an interpretation of human history (as distinct from the naïve understanding of the immediate experience of human history) in the light of an abstraction we call God.

In his book, *Thinking Straight* (1975), Antony Flew quoted a passage from Schneider and Gullans' *Last Letters from Stalingrad* (1965). "In his last letter to his wife one of the doomed soldiers of the German Sixth Army outside Stalingrad wrote: 'If there is a God, you wrote to me in your last letter, then he will bring you back to me soon and healthy. . . . But, dearest, if your words are weighed now . . . you would have to make a difficult and great decision. . . .'"[2] The decision that the soldier's wife had to make was to choose between accepting the naïve understanding that would accompany the news of her husband's death or a theoretical understanding based on a theological interpretation of the data of human history. Since these two understandings would be in conflict with each other, it was "a difficult and great decision" indeed.

To some extent the difficulties inherent in religious understanding are familiar to us. Particularly in Christianity, a strong historical dimension led from the start to the development of some degree of disillusion and doubt among the early believers. Their vision of the coming of the Kingdom of Heaven was not fulfilled during their lifetime as they expected that it would be. The passage of the first millenium, and then of the second, created doubt regarding the possibility of the Second Coming becoming an historical event. This is one of many examples of "naïve doubt" which may be compared to the "naïve belief" many intelligent non-scientists and some scientists hold with regard to science.

Viewed from the outside at a distance, basic science or natural philosophy seems like a well-organized enterprise sometimes compared to a cathedral under construction. All of the workers seem to know what they are doing; all of the completed parts of the edifice seem to be nicely arranged with respect to the others; and where the work is clearly unfinished, professionals are scrabbling around the walls, fitting data together in what seems from this distance to be a well-ordered architectural plan.

On a closer look, some of the newer parts of the structure are seen not to fit together. But this is not a cause for despair, for there is The Method, a hypothetico-deductive process that has guaranteed success for over three hundred years. Examination of any scientific paper is likely to show that the scientist made certain empirical observations which are explained in detail by a carefully worked out hypothesis suggesting certain outcomes that have, in turn, been observed or can be expected to be observed in subsequent experiments.

However, as Kuhn and others have shown, that is not the way things are. First of all, every once in a while substantial parts of the edifice begin to creak and groan and then come tumbling down. When these are rebuilt they are usually constructed in a different way, although often with the same stones. In the second place it is not unusual for many of the workers to have no idea what is the next thing to do, what is the next best question to ask.

In commenting on Bertrand Russell's description of the scientific method, Casper and Noer wrote:

> One gets the impression of a sequential process. First the facts are observed and then a hypothesis is devised. But how does one know a priori which facts are significant? . . . The difficulty arises because any physical phenomenon has associated with it a vast number of facts . . . some observations will be more significant than others . . . in the early stages of a scientific inquiry one does not yet know what the theoretical framework will be. . . . Should a theory of the planets

explain their number and the distances between them? . . .
Or should a theory explain the motions of the planets?[3]

Close examination of the history of scientific developments
shows it to be rather spasmodic or even accidental in nature, characteristics that tend to belie the idea of organized progress under
the control of a rational and deterministic scientific method. A
closer examination of science and two specific problems will reveal flaws that may not be apparent when one looks only at the
outstanding successes of scientific investigation.

Natural science, especially physics, views the world as essentially describable in terms of mathematics. It is even possible to
characterize various branches of science as more or less "mature"
in terms of the extent to which they make use of mathematical
methods of analysis. To say that the world is essentially mathematical is to claim that its behavior can be understood in terms
of analytical functions or some kind of geometric relations. The
science of mechanics and the design of machinery have progressed far on the basis of this kind of an understanding. We can
predict with great accuracy the future positions of the planets,
and we can with confidence build a loom that will turn yarns
into fabrics. The very success of celestial mechanics and mechanical design tends to blind us to the theoretical defects in our
understandings.

Now there is a curious asymmetry in theory and practice. Theoretical scientists have a tendency to underestimate what one
can build as distinct from what one can know. The asymmetry
separates scientists from inventors. Prior to the beginning of the
twentieth century scientists had shown that powered human
flight was a theoretical impossibility. It took two bicycle repair
men at Kitty Hawk to make it a reality. During the Second
World War, a Nobel prize-winning physicist gave a speech in
which he claimed to be able to show that a nuclear chain reaction was an impossibility. The speech was given only a few months
before Enrico Fermi succeeded in creating just such a sustained
nuclear chain reaction under the football stadium at the University of Chicago. It seems, then, that there is a tendency to overestimate what we think we know along with a tendency to underestimate what we can do. The effect of the interaction of

these two aspects of scientific activity is to mitigate the latter at the expense of an aggravation of the former. That is to say that our occasional unexpected successes in practice tend to cause us to overestimate still further the extent to which we know on the theoretical level. It therefore becomes necessary to look rather closely at some understandings to perceive their limitations so that they will contribute to an increased modesty with respect to our theoretical capabilities. Two examples will be considered: one form of this necessity may be cited from the realm of classical mechanics and another from geography, disciplines whose loci are far from the more mystical realms of quantum mechanics and particle theory.

It is sometimes held that our inability to develop an effective mathematical structure in the social sciences or, even less remote, in the biological sciences is the result of the presence of a large number of variables, a large number of separate mathematical quantities all influential in the situation under study. Although there are many relevant variables, their number is not the main reason for our inability to reduce the observed situation to a mathematical idealization in closed analytical form. Three hundred years of classical mechanics leave us with an elementary but insolvable problem similar to the problem of analyzing social systems with the mathematics of analytical functions. In order to grasp the difficulty we must first examine a related problem in which a solution can be found because of a peculiar coincidence.

Consider the problem of the gravitational interaction of two bodies such as a planet and the sun or, even more appropriately, two bodies of comparable mass such as the two stars in a double-star system. Each star moves under the influence of the gravitational field of the other which, in turn, moves under the influence of the first, etc. Thus the field which controls the motion of either is itself in motion. We might therefore expect to have to know the motion of the field in order to be able to calculate the motion of the star that moves under the influence of that field. But we realize that we have a circular situation because the motion of the field is the motion of the other star which we have not yet calculated. The problem could not be solved in closed analytical form were it not for a curious coincidence (or is it merely a coincidence?). It turns out that in each half of the problem we can replace the other (moving) star with a virtual star that has a mass equal to the product of the masses of the two stars divided by the sum of their two masses (a quantity referred to as the reduced mass of the system). This substitute star is placed at the "balance" point between the two stars and remains fixed while each one of the two stars moves about the virtual star. The problem is now one of calculating, for each star, its motion in the fixed gravitational field of the virtual star. This trick of substituting an equivalent problem that we can solve for one that we cannot does not work, however, in the case of three bodies of similar masses.

If three or more comparable bodies attract each other in accordance with the classical law of gravitation, a general solution to the motion of these bodies cannot be obtained. The root difficulty that arises here, despite the fact that the laws governing this situation are entirely known, is our inability to stipulate the environment of any single body, that is, to determine the forces acting on it for a long enough interval of time to obtain a solution to its change of motion. Since each body acts on every other body we have a completely interactive system. The force on any body depends on the position of all other bodies each of whose position is constantly changing under the influence of all of the other bodies.

Now it is possible to make progress towards a solution to this problem by using numerical iterative techniques in an approximation, but this is equivalent to abandoning the mathematical model in its analytical form. The numerical approach comes close to reducing the description of the system to a sequence of possible observations such as one would find in ephemeris tables. This is Babylonian science, not Greek science, and the numerical approach does not, by itself, pretend to advance our understanding of the phenomena under consideration. The Babylonians used their tables of observational data as a means of determining the regularities that made it possible to make accurate predictions of the time of occurrence of celestial events such as occultations and eclipses. However, in the absence of a model of the heavens, they could not have "reached through" the data toward the theoretical understanding. Such a restriction effectively precludes the possiblity of higher level theory such as that represented by Newton's generalization of Kepler's understanding or Einstein's generalization of Newton's.

The second example of the breakdown of idealization relates to the concept of perimeter as it arises in geography. What do we mean by the perimeter of an island? How long is the coast of Madagascar? In dealing with an object of this kind it is natural to turn to geometry, storehouse of our concepts relating to land measurement. Suppose that Madagascar were in some idealized shape, say that of an ellipse. We could then proceed to measure its perimeter by measuring its major and minor axes and calculating. But we realize that since Madagascar is not an ellipse, this method is not satisfactory. Let us weaken our assumption and say simply that Madagascar is a kind of oval. We might then go about measuring its perimeter by taking a measuring stick and measuring from one point on the perimeter to another, approximating the oval with a many-sided polygon. The perimeter of the polygon is, of course, the length of the measuring stick times the number of times that it was laid down around the edge, and we know that this is not actually the length of the perimeter of the oval. If we reduce the length of the measuring stick and repeat the process, when we multiply the new (shorter) stick length by the (larger) number of times it was laid down, we arrive at a measurement of the length of the perimeter which is closer to the perimeter of the oval.

The result of a sequence of such measurements with shorter and shorter measuring sticks might be expected to look like curve A in Fig. 3.1. Here we can see that as the length of the measuring stick approaches zero, the measurement of the length of the perimeter of the oval approaches a limiting value which we can with assurance call the length of the perimeter. This is the expectation that results from our idealization of the concept "length of the coastline of Madagascar." A measurement of the kind we have described above is just what an English scientist, L. F. Richardson, undertook. In a paper published in 1961, he showed that when we actually make such measurements on a map we do not get the result that we might expect from our idealization of a coastline into a geometrical shape with a perimeter.[4] His measurements resulted in a curve like the one shown as B in Fig. 3.1. In this case the length of the perimeter continues to increase without limit as the length of the measuring stick gets smaller—increases, we repeat for emphasis, without limit. That is, the length of the perimeter of Madagascar is infinite! What a boon to real-estate dealers who want to sell beach frontage! No, the situation is not quite like that. As the measuring stick gets smaller and smaller, we measure the "length" of each little cove along the beach, then the "length" of the curve of the water around each rock, then the "length" the edge of the water makes as it goes into each niche in each rock and round each pebble on the beach and then around each grain of sand, etc., etc. The "length" defined in this way gets longer and longer without end.

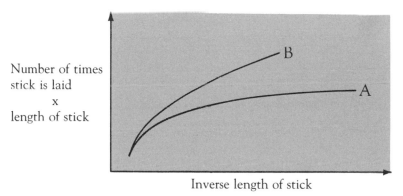

Number of times stick is laid
x
length of stick

Inverse length of stick

Fig. 3.1 A graph of the results of measuring the length of the perimeter of an oval with shorter and shorter measuring sticks. The measured perimeter length is given by the vertical axis and the inverse of the length of the measuring stick is given by the horizontal axis.

Here we have experienced the breakdown of an applied geometrical concept, that of the length of the perimeter. We have a special problem to solve because an explanatory conjugate, as Lonergan would call it, has collapsed. We need a new one.

Our story could stop here because we have illustrated the difficulty we set out to describe. However, curiosity, spurred by the normal human dissatisfaction with an unanswered question, may be demanding to know how this weird problem in geometrical geography has been solved. B. B. Mandelbrot, a computer scientist who deals with geometrical problems, has defined a new dimension to describe curves of infinite length that enclose finite areas.[5] These special curves, called fractal curves, have the same shape no matter how much they are magnified. They are useful in studying a wide range of physical shapes including not only coastlines but snowflakes, star clusters, and cloud formations.

Natural philosophy may now seem a hopeless enterprise, just as some have claimed that religion is. On the one hand, theoretical understandings take precedence over the naïve understanding of immediate experience and on the other, theoretical understanding can collapse in the face of experience. The question of how progress is made despite this inauspicious situation will be taken up in the next chapter.

• •

An informed understanding of science will dispel some of the false notions concerning its procedures, the application of its theoretical understandings, and the certainty with which its conclusions are held.

Many of the false notions regarding contemporary science can be traced back to earlier assumptions. In the seventeenth century, for example, an epistemological model of scientific knowledge was developed. In what has become a classic on religion and science, *Science and the Modern World* (1925), Alfred North Whitehead examined this model, the theory of primary and secondary qualities. He described how John Locke and other seventeenth-century thinkers cordoned off those products of human perception which appeared to be quantifiable by means of mathematics. These products were regarded as determining (primary) characteristics of objects, characteristics such as substance, space, time, and mass. All other experienced aspects of objects, aspects such as color, sound, and heat, were regarded as accidental (secondary) aspects of human perception. Whitehead called this view of science the "Fallacy of Misplaced Concreteness."[6] Only primary qualitites, "the essential qualities of substances whose spatio-temporal relationships constitute nature," were taken to be concrete. Secondary qualities, according to the theory, "in reality do not belong to objects, and . . . are purely the offspring of the mind."

The legacy of this theory is that contemporary science is concerned only with primary qualities since secondary qualities are understood to be inherent not in objects but in minds. Whitehead paraphrased Locke as follows:

> . . . nature gets credit which should in truth be reserved for ourselves; the rose for its scent: the nightingale for his song. . . . The poets are entirely mistaken. They should address their lyrics to themselves, and should turn them into odes of self-congratulation on the excellency of the human mind. Nature is a dull affair, soundless, scentless, colourless; merely the hurrying of material, endlessly, meaninglessly.[7]

The fallacy consists in dispensing with the secondary characteristics of objects. Scientists are left free to be persuaded by their research that the mathematical paradigm is not only helpful for their study of nature, but a complete and permanent description. It is astonishing that this reduction of the many-facetedness of the world went as unnoticed as it did for so long.

What is equally remarkable is that the search for primary qualities (spoken of by Whitehead as "irreducible stubborn facts") in science was paralleled by a preoccupation with origins in Western religion. In reaction to the complexity of medieval religious polity and thought, seventeenth-century religious thinkers, such as the Pietists and the Puritans, turned instead to "simple" faith and historical-devotional reconstructions of homely origins. No wonder, then, that the world of science grew increasingly remote from religion: the model of scientific method not only went unchallenged from within by scientists attending merely to data reducible to primary qualities but was abandoned also from without by humanists because the method excluded secondary qualities.

In our attempt to reformulate the project of science, we have said that our capacity for disconnecting our experience of objects from our immediate, naïve understanding of them as bodies frees the objects for being understood as things. In other words, as a result of being able to distance ourselves from objects as they appear to us in their immediacy, we are able to know them in mediated ways, ways which are often communicable and, most importantly, ways which come to constitute human reality.

This ability to know objects as mediated (as things) enables us to say that science is not determined by sense-experience. Rather, the immediacy of our experience and observation of data (or of the data of instrumentation) is always in need of mediation if it is to be significant. The earlier antinomy (namely, that concerning the role of direct experiences in a mature science) is resolved only to be replaced by another: "On the one hand it seems that our theoretical understandings take precedence over the naïve understandings of immediate experience and, on the other, our theoretical understandings can collapse in the face of experience." However, a closer examination of this statement reveals the logical problem to be more dialectical than contradictory and foreshadows a resolution in what will later be referred to as the hermeneutical circle.[8]

Finally, this relation of science to experience is paralleled by the relation of theology to experience. Corresponding to scientific observations are the reports of religious experiences put forward by religious believers. The understanding of these reports requires mediation based on an acceptance or rejection of traditional religious forms. The capacity for distancing oneself from both the immediacy of religious experiences and the special pleas that are made concerning them frees us to ignore what may be peculiarly parochial views of religious experience and to arrive at more adequate conceptions of the way things are. In other words, one must recognize how the surpassings and negativities of ordinary experience (as seen in the example of the letter written to the soldier's wife) drive us beyond our simple naïve understandings and beyond the vagaries of history. The problem becomes one of appropriately conceiving of the great inescapabilities that make our simple, naïve faith in existence at times all but impossible. It is the task of theology—which, like science, is necessarily distanced from the immediacy of faith and the special claims of any particular religious tradition—to address this problem.

RELIGION IS MORE THAN IT SEEMS

The "god of the gaps" was a phrase coined originally in the 1950's to express the idea that because science is constantly progressing in its questions about the universe, religious mystery (i.e., God) must reside in the gaps—what remains still to be known. Later the phrase was turned to theological advantage by such thinkers as Ian Ramsey who insisted that the human subject is as much a mystery as is the universe and who claimed that the "gap" therefore can never be "filled" by scientific explanation.[9]

The "god of the gaps" quickly became a cliché, but one of the central issues it raised remains: Is there continuity of data between the study of science and the study of religion? In the popular understanding of science as object-oriented and religion as subject-oriented, it is assumed that the data of science and the data of religion are radically disjointed. In this common-sense point of view, it is the "nature" of religion to identify with the individual, even the idiosyncratic. And from the same perspective, it is the "nature" of science to identify with all real understanding. One speaks of Julia(n) of Norwich's method of spirituality, because it is assumed that it is couched in the personal and idiosyncratic; by the same token, one does not speak of Newton's method of scientific discovery because it is assumed to be the only scientific method. Our task, then, is to show that there are theoretical frameworks for religious understanding and that there is more than one theoretical framework for scientific understanding. At the same time we must prevent any one framework from being understood as merely idiosyncratic and esoteric.

Methods For Understanding

Of all the philosophical approaches to the understanding of religion, the transcendental method and the hermeneutical method are more suited to our work than other philosophical approaches such as process thought, existentialism, or phenomenology (which we employed for the notion of experience in chapter two). Transcendental philosophy focuses on the general conditions for religious understanding as distinct from one or another religious theme or concept, while hermeneutical philosophy treats the relations between texts and world and links general issues of interpretation of specific themes.

We have already encountered one kind of transcendental method in Lonergan's model for the operations of consciousness in the preceding chapter. In that context, transcendental method is a structured intelligible set of terms and relations that, as Lonergan says, "it may be well to have about when it comes to describing reality or forming hypotheses."[10] But it is not a prescription to be followed for the purpose of duplicating results. It is transcendental in the sense that it explicates how a human subject is implicated whenever there is a known object, thereby providing grounds for the premise that there is no object except in the presence of subject. Lonergan's transcendental method is useful to "have about" when the question of method in religious inquiry arises. The transcendental method can be found underlying every other method and approach within the field of religion, whether historical, psychological, or literary. It is a way of accounting for the affirmations and negations of things or states of affairs that result from certain ways of understanding religious experience.

Just as Lonergan's transcendental method refined the concept of objectivity, Karl Rahner's transcendental method (which he calls "foundations") can refine the concept of subjectivity. In this way, we proceed from a study of objectivity to an understanding of subjectivity, not in the classical or Kantian sense, but in a dialectical sense in which each concept informs the other. This procedure is somewhat parallel to the way in which the dawning of Helen Keller's self-consciousness, presented in the film *The Miracle Worker*, came only after she became conscious of the meaning of objects. In order to better appreciate the interdependence of the concepts of subjectivity and objectivity, we will apply Rahner's explication of subjectivity to the question raised in the previous chapter: In what sense is there a subject only in the presence of an object? Rahner's concept of subjectivity can help us better understand what transcendence means in relation to human consciousness in both a philosophical and a religious sense.

But first we need to have a grasp of the incommensurability in the relations between our experiences and our expressions of our experiences. Becoming aware of the continual dialectic between our lived experience and our varied and changing expressions of our understandings of our lived experience, we become also aware of the larger, more fundamental question: who and what are we? In other words, in all of our attempts to know, there is operative a fundamental idea of what it means to be human, what it means to be aware not only of the already-out-there-now-real in the world but also of self-in-the-world as intelligent, critical, and sometimes deliberate and changing. Any idea we have of being-in-world is always already after the fact of the reality of our being-in-world. At times this reality of our being-in-world is a "more original unity" than any available thematization. According to Karl Rahner, "When I love, when I am tormented by questions, this human reality is not explained without remainder by the concepts which objectify it in scientific knowledge."[11] Indeed, we may speak of such a moment in Rahner's words as an "original unity of reality and its own self-presence."[12] Any concept, then, belongs to this "original unity of reality and its own self-presence" even while it also participates in the intersubjective reality—i.e., in the networks of meanings which constitute our intersubjective reality. In other words, when we are seized by profound feeling—a sense of wonder, love, anger, hatred, benevolence—we "become" what wonder, love, anger, hatred, or benevolence is. This is to say that the experience constitutes a primal unity vis-à-vis all the networks of meanings we engage as we express the experience. Only in acts of metaphor (which Aristotle called acts of genius), perhaps, is the tension between original knowledge and its concept sufficiently sustained so that something genuinely new results.

Even in our everyday acts, however, the tension between original knowledge and its concept (which belong together and yet are not one as we noticed above) is not something static. Rahner said that the tension "has a history in two directions":

The original self-presence of the subject in the actual realization of his existence strives to translate itself more and more into the conceptual, into the objectified, into language, into communication with another. Everyone strives to tell another, especially someone he loves, what he is suffering. Consequently in this tension between original knowledge and the concept which always accompanies it there is a tendency towards greater conceptualization, towards language, towards communication, and also towards theoretical knowledge of itself.[13]

Rahner went on to say:

But there is also movement in the opposite direction within this tension. One who has been formed by a common language, and educated and indoctrinated from without, experiences clearly perhaps only very slowly what he has been talking about for a long time.[14]

In short, there are two forces that arise out of the tension that exists between the original unity of reality (together with original knowledge, whether or not expressed) and its expressed concept. One force is toward the retrieval of the original knowledge signified through the concepts which have already been designed for those moments of original unity of reality. The other force is directed toward communication through and beyond the networks of meanings into which we are born.

Rahner's explanation clarifies the notion of transcendence. First of all, in the simple and original act of knowledge, attention is focused upon some object which it encounters. In other words, at the first moment, the subject is aware, but not self-aware; the knowing subject and the act of knowing are not yet the objects of knowledge.

Fig. 3.2 illustrates the way in which the knowing subject (K_1) is situated at the "other pole" of the single relationship between the knowing subject and a known object. Rahner referred to this other pole (which we call K_1, the act of self-awareness) as a "luminous realm," within which the individual object upon which attention is focused ($K_0 \longleftrightarrow 0$) can become manifest.[15] This "luminous realm" (the self-awareness of the knower) goes unthematized (is not understood as an object of knowing) whenever the knower focuses exclusively on an external object. Rahner said that the subjective consciousness of the knower goes on, so to speak, "behind the back of the knower," who focuses away from the self in knowing the object. There is no way of escaping this indirect way that we know ourselves as knowing, even if we focus upon ourselves as the object of our inquiry. Hence, the curved arrow from ($K_0 \longleftrightarrow 0$) toward K_1 indicates the knowing subject in the act of self-awareness; the curved arrow from K_1 toward ($K_0 \longleftrightarrow 0$) indicates a return to the knowing subject, though not just the knowing subject but the knowing subject simultaneously constituted with the known object, indicated by the bi-directional arrow connecting the object to the knower conscious of the object. The successive movements to and from self-awareness form a hermeneutical circle.

Fig. 3.2 An illustration of the relationship between the awareness of an object and self-awareness. K_0 is the knower conscious of 0, an object. K_1 is the knower become self-aware, i.e., the "other" pole of an original act of knowledge.

Now transcendence is not to be found in the knowing subject. Even less likely is it to be found in the objects that are known. For, detached from the act of knowing, things quickly become stagnant formulas, capable only of being parroted and applied mechanically. Rather, transcendence arises from the disclosure of the horizon in every act of knowing. That is to say, notwithstanding the ordinary limitations of our sense perceptions, we have a basic openness for absolutely everything, for existence as such.

In other words, there are no restrictions on what might be taken as a question for the knowing subject. For example, human ears can ordinarily hear sounds only below a frequency of 20,000 Hz. Nevertheless, we can inquire into sounds that we cannot hear. Even should a person deny that we are open to being as such, beyond that which we experience, that person implicitly gives evidence that the human horizon is open. For a personal subject that knows itself to be finite is not merely unknowing with regard to the limited nature of the possibility of the objects of its knowing. Rather, by knowing itself to be finite, the subject has already transcended its immediate finiteness. What has happened here? "The subject has differentiated itself as finite from a given horizon of possible objects that is of infinite breadth. This horizon is experienced subjectively and unthematically."[16] Furthermore, should a person objectively and thematically declare, "There is no truth," such a person, in fact, affirms the statement, "There is no truth," as true. Otherwise the statement would make no sense. Rahner pointed out that "By the fact that in such an act and on its subjective pole the person necessarily affirms the existence of truth, although he does this in unthematic knowledge, he already experiences himself in possession of such a knowledge."[17] A person can legitimately affirm, therefore, that humans are open to being as such. When this horizon of being is thematized religiously, it is most often understood as the sacred, Yahweh, Allah, or God. When it is thematized philosophically and theologically, it is often also understood as the transcendent, unity, or being itself.

Rahner fomulated his concept of transcendence out of this explanation of subjectivity:

> We shall call transcendence the subjective, unthematic, necessary and unfailing consciousness of the knowing subject that is co-present in every act of knowledge, and the subject's openness to the unlimited expanse of all possible reality.[18]

It follows that "transcendence," whether religious, theological, or philosophical, is not constituted by whether or not one speaks of transcendence. Transcendence is always there, but for this reason it can nearly always be overlooked. Since transcendence is always there, we are not likely to be surprised when we advert to it. It is not like discovering a new object "out there" in the world or even a new psychological datum about oneself. Nevertheless, once a person has begun to ask about asking itself, turning attention to the scope of knowledge and not only to answers and the objects of knowledge, the person is, according to Rahner, just "on the threshold of becoming a religious person."[19]

Given this understanding of transcendence, a person will no longer consider religion to be answers revealed from "on high," that is, answers which have been given prior to any question that might be raised. As we have seen from Rahner's analysis by way of transcendental method, the questions are as important as the answers. And not only are both questions and answers important, but so also are the acts of the knowing subject who not only questions and answers but also appreciates the scope of the questioning and answering, appreciates that what we call knowledge is only "a small island in a vast sea that has not been traveled. It is a floating island," Rahner said, "and it might be more familiar to us than the sea, but ultimately it is borne by the sea and only because it is can we be borne by it." [20]

The development of a particular doctrine illustrates a hermeneutical approach to some of the foregoing issues. Some take the doctrine of christology in Christianity (i.e., that Jesus is God) to be only a literal statement—a truth, as such, revealed by the already-out-there-now-real God and therefore having nothing to do with human history and transcendence, except by accommodation. In other words, for the literalist, the constant is the already-out-there-now-real God, and humans are only coincidental recipients of the gift of "His Son." In fact, however, the doctrine of christology grew out of first century reflections on the new burgeoning of religious spirit centered on God's manifestation in Jesus of Nazareth. The originating meanings in christology were mediated by Hebraic meanings, for example, of "messiah," and were based on beliefs, images, and institutions of that time.

The doctrine of christology was finally shaped and defined for the first time at the Council of Nicea (325 C.E.). [21] There the major question was the status of the Word, as Jesus is called in the Platonic Gospel of John, in relation to the Godhead. This question had grown out of a concern for the divine unity of God. There was a need to clarify the classical references to Father, Son, and Spirit found in the Hebrew and Christian testaments because dissension had arisen regarding the way "Son" was to be understood. These were the questions being asked at the Council of Nicea: Is Christ fully divine and co-eternal with the Father? Is he really kin to the Father? And the formalized answers, which became doctrinal, often without historical context, were as follows: Yes, Christ is fully divine and he exists from the beginning of time with the Father. Yes, he is the Son of the Father.

But dissension continued and 125 years later it was necessary to call another council, at Chalcedon, (451 C.E.),[22] again on the question of christology because another set of questions had arisen: Is Christ fully human and like us? Does he really exist as a human being? (Notice that the Nicean and Chalcedonian questions complement each other.) And again formalized answers were agreed upon: Yes, Christ possesses a human body. And yes, he is equally of human as well as divine nature. In other words, in both councils, there were manifest explicit questions and answers (or concepts) which were formulated under the pressure of new historical situations, reflecting original knowledge possessed by the participants and/or the understandings of testamental witnesses. According to Monika Hellwig, the fifth century christological definition was "a cautious naming of the unknown in Christian experience of divine intervention."[23]

Both before and after these two councils, there arose many questions and answers about the understanding of the Christ in relation to God or the sacred. One solution is particularly interesting to us because it takes the act of knowing, the knower, and the known, and embodies them in a theoretical model for the nature of God. In the fifth century, in an attempt to express systematically the doctrines of God and of Christ, Augustine of Hippo understood the Father as the knower who from all time created all objects and who also thought (or conceived) the Word, or the Logos which was his Son Jesus, in whom all objects have their meaning. The Spirit, proceeding from both Father and Son, was understood by Augustine as the known, that is, the mutual knowing of the Father and the Son by each other. Embedded in classical concepts, such as nature, hypostases, substance, and essence, is an epistemological model for what Rahner called transcendence, "the unthematic necessary and unfailing consciousness of the knowing subject that is co-present in every act of knowledge."[24]

It is now apparent that Lonergan's operations of consciousness and the question of transcendence are involved in both the scientist's and the theologian's cognitive activities. Most simply stated: in the cognitive order, being aware surpasses being inattentive; being intelligent surpasses being stupid; being critical surpasses being naïve; being deliberate surpasses drifting solely by whim or fancy. Cognitive self-transcendence can be found in those who are attentive, intelligent, critical and decisive.

David Tracy shows further how cognitive self-transcendence is related to religious self-transcendence when a human subject becomes aware of limit-questions which can be discovered in reflections at each level of consciousness.[25] On the level of understanding, the inquirer eventually asks what makes the particular object under investigation intelligible—i.e., questions the ground of intelligibility. On the level of judgment, the inquirer eventually asks the value of the critical inquiry itself. And on the level of decisive action, the inquirer is brought eventually to the question of ultimate values—should all else fail, for what would I live or die? Limit-questions occur, for Tracy, also in the course of moral deliberations. There are, for example, no moral arguments for being moral: rather, one finds oneself compelled to say something about a basic trust and confidence or the lack thereof to be found in the very structures of experience.

Transcendence, then, is a threshold experience. It results from going beyond the world of the everyday where common sense reigns. We cross the threshold of cognitive self-transcendence whenever we shape our worlds by means of careful and imaginative differentiations. We cross the threshold of moral self-transcendence whenever our actions shape ourselves by means of critical reflection. We cross the threshold of religious self-transcendence whenever the limits of our own achievements raise ultimate questions, to which ultimate answers may or may not exist, may or may not be given, may or may not be found.

• •

By making objective the subjective pole of human cognition, we find a way to explicate the process of coming-to-know, a process which forms common ground for both religion and science. Transcendental method has made it possible to achieve a focus on the relationship between the knowing subject and the knower-knowing-the-known. We are, in a manner of speaking, raised above our own selves in our own environment. As if in a dream, we seem to "observe" our knowing selves: we now ask not about method as disembodied process but rather about method as a human activity which incorporates a human subject. We imagine the scientist or ourselves "down there" doing science. And we come to a clearer understanding that the scientific method is a process that involves the cognitive acts of that scientist or ourselves. Criticism now becomes self-criticism and we find the renewed focus on the questioner and the questions.

"Should a theory of the planets account for their motion or their number?" asked Johannes Kepler. As we read of Kepler's struggle to understand the solar system we encounter at first a mathematician who was convinced beyond all reason that the planetary orbits correspond to a nested set of the five Platonic "perfect" solids and therefore the question was "How many planets?"[26] Then, later, as his efforts to match the orbits to his model proved unfruitful, his conviction gradually weakened, and he began to ask new questions about the shapes of the orbits and the speed of the motion. The question became, "How do planets move?" Was there a K_1, a reflecting Kepler, who was conscious of $(K_0 \longleftrightarrow 0)$, the Kepler struggling with the planets? Did Kepler at any time enter a state of self-transcendence that made it possible for him to think reflectively: "Here I am trying to understand the system of the planets and I have been trying to fit their orbits into a set of spheres that nest inside each other and whose sizes are determined by the sequence of the five perfect Platonic solids that just fit within them. Perhaps I have been trying to answer the wrong question. Perhaps I should be trying to develop a model that will explain how the planets move." Since Kepler did not report any such inner thoughts, we cannot know that he ever had them. It might seem, then, that the transcendental model of consciousness described earlier is of little use since we can rarely know enough about a subject to be able to verify subjective experiences of this kind. However, to argue this way is to miss the point. We are not being asked to verify any experience of Kepler's. What we seek to do is to verify our understanding of such an experience insofar as such an experience can become known by us.

We are now clearly conscious that there are limits to our understanding of subjectivity and limits to our understanding of the thoughts and questions of theologians and natural philosophers. The transcendental method would seem to provide a basis for interpreting what little information is available about intellectual processes that take place at the forefronts of science and religion.

Fortunately, we have a few instances of creative individuals who not only thought about the objects of their concerns but also reflected on the way in which they came to understand these objects. We know this because their reflections on process were recorded and are available for us. Saul of Tarsus, who became the Apostle Paul, and Albert Einstein are two such examples. We will consider their thoughts in a later chapter.

For now we can say that we are prepared to examine the way in which a theologian or natural scientist deals with what is known. Our awareness of the transitory character of much that we claim to know, coupled with the perspective on the knowing subject that is provided by the idea of self-transcendence, makes it possible for us to examine, now, the way in which knowledge grows and changes and the reasons why the understandings that we achieve are surrendered so reluctantly.

CHAPTER FOUR

Knowledge-In-Process

THE CASUAL OBSERVER of science and religion must wonder at the sometimes subtle, sometimes stormy balance that is maintained between permanence and change within each of the two disciplines. How meanings break up or emerge on the edges of the two fields, how some meanings are perennially affirmed and extended, how others fall into desuetude—these are the problems we address in this chapter.

STABLE KNOWLEDGE: MYTH OR REALITY?

Robert Bly, a well-known contemporary American poet, occasionally dons a mask during his poetry readings. Wearing the mask of selected stereotypical men or women, he impersonates certain staid views of our world. Common to all of these impersonations, he maintains, is antipathy to change. Bly contrasts the degenerative dreams of his masked persona with what he calls "being awake"; he contends that moments of being awake and persons who are frequently awake are both rare. "Being really awake can't happen before you're thirty-five," he asserts. To be sure, there can be some small flashes of awareness before then but to be dynamically cognizant of our integral worlds, Bly thinks, takes a long time.[1]

Bly is being rhetorical and persuasive rather than empirical or literal, at least about the frequency of such moments. Nevertheless, his putting the issue of awareness under the general notion of temporality is closely related to the common understanding of myth. Earl MacCormac, for example, pointed out that we can recognize a myth only after it has been replaced.[2] He claimed that at any given time it may be possible to sort out literal under-standings from theoretical ones, thus preventing the reification of meaning that he took to be a characteristic of myth. Both Bly's dramatization of what it means to be "awake," and MacCormac's analysis of what it means to be current and non-literal, however, give rise to certain further questions. Is it true that every the-oretical meaning that has been replaced by another meaning is a myth? How is it possible to distinguish between a literal and a theoretical understanding without reference to the person under-standing the object in question? What relation does our under-standing of that which is abstract have to our understanding of that which is concrete?

In order to take up these questions, a more detailed epis-temological framework is needed. Particularly useful will be the concept of "horizon-analysis." Our investigation of science and religion has demonstrated that knowledge is always in process whether we are referring to fields of meaning in general or to par-ticular fields of meanings for individual knowers. If change in meaning, as distinct from permanence of meaning, is the starting point of analysis, the major problem becomes one of accounting for the way in which meanings constitute an affirmed reality at any given moment in history.

Knowledge-in-process for the individual knower is best under-stood in terms not of how the answers change but how the ques-tions do. An individual's horizon, according to Lonergan, has a three-fold range:[3] There are questions which I ask and answer (this is the range of the known-known); next, there are questions which I ask and can even propose ways of solving but cannot in fact yet answer (this is the range of the known-unknown); finally there are questions that I do not raise because they are not mean-ingful to me. I know about this last range of questions, the un-known-unknown, because I can remember the experience of rais-ing a new question which had never occurred to me before, or because others ask questions which I do not initially but only later come to understand. If we define horizon as the limit of that which I can understand from a known perspective, then my hori-zon would seem to be between the second and third range of questions just referred to (between the known-unknown and the unknown-unknown). In this sense, horizons are like myths; we do not have any sense of the range of our questions until we have transcended our present horizon. In a similar way, we may be unaware that we have literalized a particular understanding until another appears to show that what we took to be a final reality can be more comprehensively understood another way.[4]

In the disciplines of science and religion, knowledge-in-process is best perceived in historical horizon-shifts, that is, in the occurrence of new and significantly distinct forms of understanding. For example, we recognize in retrospect the emergence of theoretical thought in fifth century B. C. E. Athens; the development of empirical canons in twelfth- and thirteenth-century Oxford; the emergence of "critical" philosophy in eighteenth-century Germany. Other examples can be added: the rise of monotheistic theology in ancient Judaism; the mid-twentieth-century indigenization of Eastern religions in Europe and America; the late twentieth-century invention of computer technology and artificial intelligence. In each of these instances, new forms of understanding give evidence of a horizon-shift. New questions begin to be asked and are mediated within new fields of meanings. Mediation here refers to the process by which new questions become meaningful and, in many instances, even definitive of new forms of self-awareness.

By attempting to understand science and religion in the context of horizon-shifts (that is, by tracing the shifts in all of their manifestations from their origin, through the integration of influences in different fields, to the height of their expression in classical forms), we begin to see that certain correlations between science and religion can be made at any given major historical period. Some generalists assume that scientific explanations began, in the Renaissance, to replace religious beliefs. Instead of an assumption which eliminates either science or religion, what is needed, however, is a more penetrating understanding of their inter-relationship in any given epoch. Even historians of science and religion come close to being naïve on this point. MacCormac, too, seemed to imply the substitution of scientific explanation for religious stories when he stated,

Contemporary men rightly assume that modern scientific explanations are superior to stories about deities as descriptions of how the world operates, for we have accumulated more corroboratory evidence for the former that also falsifies the latter.[5]

And later on he asserted,

> The difference between the stories which the Vedas offer for the creation of the world and the theories of modern science about the origin of the world may seem vast, so vast that we want to call the former superstitious and the latter a rational explanation. Yet, for primitive men, myths were the only explanations they had. . . .[6]

Instead of sweeping contrasts between contemporary science and primitive religion we need careful comparisons of the scientific and religious thinking of primitive people on the one hand and the scientific and religious dimensions of contemporary understanding on the other.

Meaning is said to be constitutive when it has become stabilized for any given generation. Stabilized meanings are mediated (i.e., communicated in the sense of meaningful questions which are for the most part satisfactorily answered) and become embodied in the culture, institutions and technology. In other words, as embodied, these affirmed meanings constitute reality for most people at that particular time. The stabilization of meanings (as distinct from an ossification of meaning) does not by itself cause naïveté. Nor does the stabilization of meanings necessarily correspond to the literalization of theoretical understandings, as Mac-Cormac's analysis seems to imply. One might even argue to the contrary: When meanings are unstable, one's horizon of understanding as previously constituted may be so threatened that one may, out of fear, reject theoretical understandings.

For any individual, the experiencing and understanding of knowledge-in-process means the avoidance of two kinds of naïveté.[7] The first kind results from the failure to ask questions about our experiences and observations. The person dominated by first naïveté is confined to reacting and submitting to that which always seems already-out-there-now-real. The second kind of naïveté is more difficult to discover in oneself.[8] It results from the failure to ask questions about one's questions. The person dominated by second naïveté makes no distinction between questions that can be asked and answered and those that can be asked but not answered and never remembers the experience of beginning to be able to ask a new question not thought of before. We might say that second naïveté is constituted by an ignorance of the process by which one comes to know. A consciousness characterized by second naïveté concentrates on grasping what appear to be the fixities of theoretical understandings. The contrast between knowledge-in-process and the two kinds of naïveté is illustrated in Fig. 4.1.

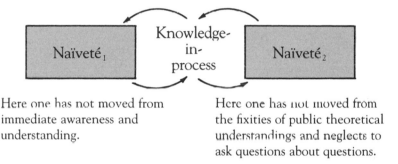

Here one has not moved from immediate awareness and understanding.

Here one has not moved from the fixities of public theoretical understandings and neglects to ask questions about questions.

Fig. 4.1 An illustration of the contrast between knowledge-in-process and two kinds of naïveté.

The individual ought not to fear naïveté if engaged in overcoming it. Although the discovery of naïveté in oneself is threatening, frustrating and even embarrassing, it becomes a reliable indicator for a horizon-shift that otherwise might have gone unnoticed. Naïveté is likely to occur whenever one encounters a new or significantly different object of experience. Naïveté occurs whenever one holds assumptions about a field of meaning, assumptions which are shown to be too simple or inadequate in the face of further evidence. Discovery of this kind of naïveté discloses something different to be learned about an object or state of affairs previously taken for granted and becomes a most effective way of prodding ourselves out of our dogmatic slumbers.

Specifying the two kinds of naïveté makes possible the perception of instances of naïveté in oneself as well as in one's worlds. Consider the kinds of questions that impel one toward knowledge-in-process: To what extent does one live within a Newtonian or Einsteinian world view in science? To what extent does one live within an essentialist, a transcendental, or a process world view in theology? To what extent is one's self-understanding appropriate and authentic?

Such an understanding of naïveté provides responses to the three other questions raised earlier. In response to the question, "Is it proper to call every theoretical understanding that has been replaced by another a myth?" we can now reply: No, myth ought to refer only to those theoretical understandings which have lost their hypothetical dimension, that is, only to those which cease to be rooted in knowledge-in-process and which categorically exclude the possibly of further questions relating to the hypothesis. Second, in response to the question, "How is it possible to distinguish between a literal and a theoretical understanding without reference to the person understanding an object in question?" we can reply: Strictly speaking, there is no way to distinguish between a literal and a theoretical understanding without a horizon-analysis of the subject persisting in the understanding. However, since we have no direct access to the interior, we make informed guesses with respect to any specific understanding and then reconstruct it as best we can. We call this process of informed guessing and reconstruction "interpretation"; it comprises most of human knowing.

Finally, in response to the last question, "What relation does a theoretical understanding have to reality?" we may say that insofar as the "real" is what is made our own through our judgments informed by our understanding, theoretical understanding is a significant part of what constitutes reality for an individual, a community of individuals, a generation, an epoch, or for all humanity. In this sense, it is one's constitution of (as distinct from one's view of) reality that involves a personal commitment and is a manifest source of all one's judgments. Knowledge-in-process is, then, a crucial condition for the authenticity of stable meanings. Later, we shall see that it is a condition for the emergence of new meaning as well.

• •

Lonergan's analysis shows us one way of assessing our cognitive states. "Am I asking questions?" we ask. If we answer that we are not, we may be in a state of first naïveté. "Have I considered whether the questions I am asking are the right questions?" we ask further. If we answer, "No," again we may be in a state of second naïveté. In either case we are in a kind of cognitive backwater, out of the main stream of active knowing.

While such horizon-analysis will prove valuable to our effort to understand the cognitive process, it leaves several questions unanswered. For example, if I am in a state of doubt it might seem that I am questioning my understandings even though I have not formulated any question about these understandings. It would seem, therefore, that a person could avoid second naïveté by considering everything to be doubtful. Is the skeptic immune to horizon-analysis? Perhaps the answer is found in emphasizing the character of the questions that are raised. If the emphasis is on the kind of question rather than on the fact of doubt, then we will understand that doubt itself does not suffice to move us into the main stream of cognitive development.

We have stressed the importance of the choice of question in science, since it would seem that, while the acknowledgement of ignorance may be a first step to the growth of the intellect, the choice of question has a strong influence on the probability of successful enlargement of our world of meanings.

Returning to the issue of overcoming either first or second naïveté, we find that horizon-analysis is a process by which we recognize both limitations and achievements in ourselves. Most of our data showing knowledge-in-process in science and religion relate to this process as it takes place in individuals. However, we must not think of horizon-analysis as applying merely to ourselves and others as individuals. Once we understand the way our own understandings develop, we are better able to understand both the horizon-shifts that take place within other knowers and the horizon-shifts that occur for entire fields of meanings. Moreover, the horizon of an entire field of meanings is not coincident with the sum of the most distant horizons of all of the individuals who represent that field. Requirements of intersubjectivity on the one hand and the existence of knowledge which cannot be shared on the other, virtually guarantee that the knowledge of all of the scientists in the world, for example, is greater than the knowledge that can be said to comprise the field of meanings identified as science. Although a horizon-shift in one scientist is not equivalent to a horizon-shift for all science, the transfer of our understanding of the process of coming-to-know in ourselves leads to an understanding, by analogy, of that process in other individuals and in entire fields of knowledge.

There is a routine that is sometimes seen on a late-night television talk-show in which Karmac, the master of ceremonies, holds a sealed envelope to his head and says, "The answer is . . ." after which he gives an answer. The envelope is then opened and the question is read. The question invariably turns out to be not what was expected, much to the delight of the audience.

In a curious way our task is similar to the task of Karmac on that television show. We have some of the answers that have been found by scientists and theologians. We do not intuit the answers; they usually reside in the writings of these persons. What we do not know, just as Karmac and the audience do not know, is what the questions were. And here an understanding of first and second naïveté and the way in which they relate to horizon growth may prove to be valuable. The answers of others are inferential clues to the questions and the cognitive processes of others, if our understanding of these processes is sufficiently well developed.

At the outset of our investigation of the relationship between science and religion we said that we rejected any comparison of these two human activities on the basis of the objects with which they seem to be dealing and would focus our attention rather on the way in which natural philosophers or theologians come to know that which they claim to know. Our investigation has now reached the stage where it would seem to be possible to dispense with some of the simpler models for the acquisition of knowledge in either field. First of all, we can say that the growth of knowledge should not be thought of as a more or less steady accretion of information or even of theories. Both in science and religion old truths do not last forever. We might next think that the growth of knowledge could be understood as the replacement of old knowledge by new knowledge, i.e., the answers to questions. The fact is, however, that theoretical understandings have a tenacity that belies this simple model, and so it is to this question of the resilience of ideas that we now turn.

WHY THEORIES LAST

In the introduction to his book, *Thematic Origins of Scientific Thought* (1973), Gerald Holton pointed out important differences between what he called "public science" or "S_2," and "private science" or "S_1."[9] Operationally, public science or S_2 is conducted on a two-dimensional plane, which Holton called the contingent plane with x- and y-axes, "in which a scientific concept or a scientific proposition has both empirical [x] and analytical [y] relevance." For a more complete analysis, however, he recommended a three-dimensional space, which could include those "preconceptions which appear to be unavoidable for scientific thought, but are themselves not verifiable or falsifiable"—preconceptions which are ordinarily relegated to private science or S_1. For this purpose he defined a third, z-axis, perpendicular to the x-y plane and having to do with an orthogonal dimension he called "thematic." In this third dimension, Holton found

> an active and necessary component that is effective in scientific work. . . . There we are more likely to see plainly the illogical, non-linear, and therefore "irrational" elements that are juxtaposed to the logical nature of the concepts themselves. Cases abound that give evidence of the role of "unscientific" preconceptions, passionate motivations, varieties of temperament, intuitive leaps, serendipity or sheer bad luck, not to speak of the incredible tenacity with which certain ideas have been held despite the fact that they conflicted with the plain experimental evidence.[10]

It is this latter effect, the perseverance of ideas in the face of contrary evidence, that we wish to focus on. How does this come about? What justification does a scientist have for such irrational behavior? Is not science an open-minded search for truth pursued in an objective and dispassionate way? Apparently it is not, and if we are to begin to understand what it means to know in science and compare this to what it means to know in religion, it will be necessary for us to do some probing beyond Holton's contingent plane into the S_1 of private science.

Before beginning this exploration we wish to reassert what we said earlier lest there be at this point a significant misunderstanding. We said that we would not be considering private knowledge in either science or religion, i.e., knowledge that is in some sense incommunicable and hence forever closed to the world of discourse. However, we must do more than examine the oh's! and ah's! of ecstatic experience if we are to begin to understand why it is that an idea can gain such a grip on a human being. Accordingly we will consider some of the characteristics of the "nascent moment" first as it occurs in science.[11]

The paradigmatic example of the "nascent moment" or the "disclosure" as Ian Ramsey called it, is Archimedes' sudden realization, in the midst of a bath, that he could determine the volume of an irregular object by immersing it in water. So overjoyed was he at this "revelation" that, we are told, he ran naked through the street crying "Eureka! I have it!" (all in Greek, of course). An experience of this kind has been of special interest to scholars in many different fields. It has been been given a variety of names from "peak-experience" (Maslow), and "disclosure situation" (Ramsey), to "limit-experience" (Tracy).[12] For our purposes it is important to relate such an experience to the experiences we have described thus far.

To distinguish the nascent moment from immediate experience which carries a naïve understanding with it, it will be useful to develop a graphic model of the special experience by means of Venn diagrams. These are closed curves drawn in a plane, curves that enclose areas that correspond, in mathematical situations, to sets. When such closed curves intersect it is understood that there are elements in each set that are held in common. Venn diagrams help us understand, in certain situations, just what the relations between things are, what elements are included and what excluded.

We begin with two curves as in Fig. 4.2a. The larger is considered to represent a person's world of meanings (W). The second small circle is a percept (P), a stimulus to the person's sensory system. There is no intersection between the two. We say that there is no understanding in this case, either because the person is unaware of the percept or because the percept has no "meaning" (a rare situation).

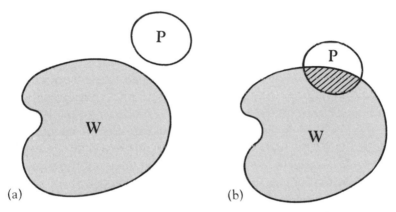

Fig. 4.2 An illustration of immediate experience which carries a naïve understanding. (a) The world of meanings does not intersect with a percept and hence does not yield understanding. (b) The world of meanings does intersect with a percept and yields naïve understanding.

Fig. 4.2b shows a similar arrangement except that now there is an intersection between the two curves. This diagram corresponds to the naïve (unmediated) understanding of immediate experience. The double-shaded area common to both the world of meanings (already held) and the perception corresponds to what we mean by the understanding. Naïve understanding is entirely contained within the original world of meanings so that the latter is neither changed nor enlarged by the experience.

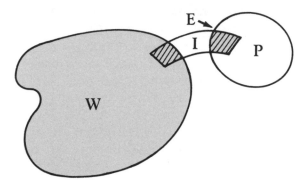

Fig. 4.3 An illustration of the result of mediation between experience and understanding.

The next example, shown as Fig. 4.3, illustrates the situation that results when there is mediation between experience and understanding, for example, the case of the scientist examining data and beginning to interpret. This experience of interpretation (I) is distinguished from the immediate experience of data (an experience which is unmediated) by the addition of a third strip that intersects both the world of meanings and the perception. The result of these intersections is an enlargement (E) of the world of meanings, a growth in our theoretical understanding.

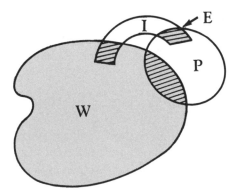

Fig. 4.4 An illustration of a naïve understanding of immediate experience and a theoretical or interpreted understanding of the same experience giving rise to contradictory understandings.

Fig. 4.4 indicates how contradictory understanding can arise when, as in the case of Brahe or Kepler, a person has a naïve understanding of immediate experience on the one hand and a theoretical or interpreted understanding of the same experience on the other. Again, there is no enlargement of the world of meanings as a result of the person's naïve understanding although there is an enlargement that results from the person's mediated understanding based on interpretation.

Can this model be applied to the situation of Archimedes pondering his problem? He has the problem formulated and he works on it in his imagination, trying different combinations and arrangements within his world of meanings. The tension begins to build as he realizes that he must reach beyond his present state of theoretical understandings. This situation is shown in Fig. 4.5a. Figure 4.5b illustrates his encounter in the bath by adding the perceptual experience to which he is not paying attention. Finally in Fig. 4.5c his world of meanings erupts and intersects the perception associated with his bath and "Eureka!" a new under-

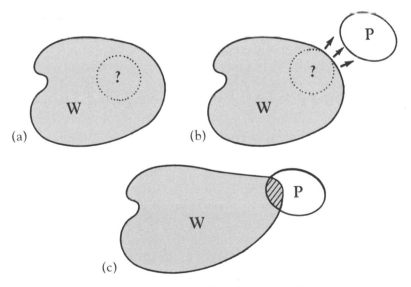

Fig. 4.5 An illustration of the birth of understanding. (a) Tension builds as problem is pondered. (b) A new perceptual experience is added. (c) The world of meaning erupts and intersects with the new perceptual experience.

standing is abruptly born. The diagram would be the same as that for a naïve understanding (4.2b) were it not for the enlargement of the world of meanings that has taken place.

What is different about this situation from the one depicted in Fig. 4.3? The end result is the same, but the means to the end are very different. In the disclosure situation, as distinct from the mediated one, there is a sudden realization as if given rather than achieved. It is this "givenness" that makes the experience what it is. It is an experience of "the other," of discovery. Not that the experience is independent of the world of meanings or the previous theoretical understandings—it just seems as if it is.

To have such a disclosure experience is to know that something is true even though one has not yet shown, by some method of analysis, that it is. This pre-knowledge, this confidence, has its parallel in certain forms of religious experience. It gives rise to what might be called the tenacity of faith, an unwillingness to abandon an idea in the face of conflicting evidence. It is similar to the faith that can arise in a personal interaction of the kind Ramsey referred to. The knowledge that one has of a friend can cause one to believe, for example, that a friend is innocent of a crime of which he or she has been accused in spite of much evidence for the truth of the accusation. So also can scientists, seen as Ramsey would see them as if in personal interchange with the universe, be understood to develop a faith in what is understood, a faith in that knowledge or in that theoretical understanding.

Nor does such strongly held belief stem only from sudden disclosures of the kind that Archimedes had. It can arise also out of a radical, sudden and complete experience of the efficacy of deduction. Recall the fallacy of assuming that a premise is shown to be true when its conclusion is observed; that is, if A implies B we cannot conclude from an observation of B that A is so. For example, if eating green apples (A) makes you sick (B), one cannot conclude that because you are sick (B), you have eaten green apples (A). However, consider how much stronger the effect of the (still fallacious) argument is if one has many interdependent premises; i.e., if A_1 and A_2 and A_3 and A_4 . . . all together imply B, then an observation of B seems overwhelming confirmation of all of the premises.

An example in its most dramatic form took place on December 2, 1942, when Enrico Fermi supervised the creation of the first nuclear chain reaction, something that some reputable physicists had said was an impossibility. His achievement was the result of countless deductive calculations based on his understanding of the interactive properties of neutrons and atomic nuclei. When the carbon control rod was withdrawn from the atomic pile under the football stadium at the University of Chicago's Stagg Field, the geiger counters indicated that the chain reaction had started and was sustained. Under these circumstances how would it have been possible for the spectators to have doubted the truth of the understandings that Fermi had? For whatever effect they may have or have had on the world, it would seem that the same could be said of Robert Oppenheimer at the first atomic bomb explosion at Alamogordo and of Edward Teller at the explosion of the first hydrogen bomb at Eniwetok.

Theoretical understandings, at least some of them, are impressively buttressed by shocking experiences of induction or striking experience of deductive efficacy. It is not surprising, then, that the understandings are given up with such reluctance if they are given up at all. As Max Planck said, "a new scientific truth does not triumph by convincing its opponents . . . [it triumphs] because its opponents die, and a new generation grows up that is familiar with it."[13]

We have, at this point, achieved two objectives: we have shown that theoretical understanding takes precedence over the naïve understanding of immediate experience and that limit-experiences are part of the life of scientific discovery. Such experiences develop, in the human being who has them, a tenacious faith that overpowers contrary evidence and sounds the battle alarm whenever contrary views are expressed. So strong can this faith be that an observer might be forced to conclude that scientists are reacting to what they perceive as heresy. And, as it is with smoke and fire, where there's heresy, there's dogma.

For example, in the spring of 1950 Immanuel Velikovski, a scholar who called himself a psycho-historian, published a book entitled *Worlds in Collision*.[14] In this volume he assembled the comparative testimony of texts from many different sources to create an argument for the existence of cataclysmic events in the past that gave rise, for example, to the planet Venus, events that he claimed had been suppressed and lost from the collective consciousness and memory. It is a wild tale, totally disconnected from the scientific paradigm that informs traditional thought in the area. The reaction of the academic community was swift. Velikovski was denounced as a charlatan and his publisher, Macmillan and Company, was put under such pressure from the Eastern academic community that it promptly dropped the book although the edition had been selling very well. This is hardly an example of the response of an open-minded community. Indeed such overkill seems to be *prima facie* evidence for the existence of a threat to dogma.

That reaction of this kind on the part of scientists continues is shown by a 1975 monograph entitled *Objections to Astrology*, in which "192 leading scientists, including 19 Nobel Prize winners, disavow astrology."[15] The "Statement by 192 Leading Scientists" concludes with the paragraph,

> It should be apparent that those individuals who continue to have faith in astrology do so in spite of the fact that there is no verified scientific basis for their beliefs, and indeed that there is strong evidence to the contrary.[16]

This statement is strikingly similar to that made by Holton, with respect to scientists, that "certain ideas have been held despite the fact that they conflicted with the plain experimental evidence."[17] What is going on here?

It appears that the 192 scientists have not only adopted a naïve epistemological perspective—one their own enterprise would not support—but they have, in addition, adopted a tone that is distinctly *ex cathedra*. It would be no surprise to find a pronouncement derived from an equivalent epistemology but of a religious nature being uttered by Spanish inquisitors in the fifteenth or sixteenth century. We are not saying that there is any truth in astrology as we know it. We are merely suggesting that the righteous attitude toward what we claim to know is strikingly similar in the case of contemporary science on the one hand and traditional religion on the other. It seems reasonable to conclude that there is a parallel between what we might call scientific faith in the first case and religious faith in the second.[18]

Some commentators on the relationship between science and religion locate the religious dimension of science exclusively in the area of the moral and ethical choices of scientists. Granting the strong interaction among questions of values, ethics, morals, and religion, it should be clear that these dimensions exist not only for scientists but for every human activity from movie producer to corporate executive. Accordingly, to search for interrelatedness between science and religion in the day-to-day lives of scientists is to imply that science has a religious dimension only because it is a human activity—an undeniable claim, but one that does not help us in our search for the relation between science as a field of meanings and religion as a field of meanings.

Merely to examine the objects with which either science or religion deals is to miss the process whereby the fields of meaning develop; it is the study of this process that is fruitful. Knowledge-in-process is human activity but always a particular kind of human activity, not just general human activity. And it is in the particularities of this human activity in science that we look to find the relatedness that we seek.

The experience of beauty in scientific knowledge can also give rise to a conviction that can amount to faith. Holton quoted P.A.M. Dirac, one of the outstanding theoretical physicists of the twentieth century, as saying, "a theory that has some mathematical beauty is more likely to be correct than an ugly one that gives a detailed fit to experiments."[19] And here we have a last criterion, still another consideration that can give theoretical understanding primacy over the naïve understanding of immediate experience. The beauty of a theory is persuasive of its truth. But the question of beauty is a limit-question, a value question, and therefore evidence of a religious dimension in science. What does it mean to say that nature is beautiful in the sense that the laws of nature have great aesthetic quality? We do not refer here to any quality of beauty that may be found in the naïve understanding of immediate experience. The goose flying into the sunset or the surf against the rocks are not the experiences of beauty that we have in mind. We refer, for example, to Gauss' Law of the relationship between electric charge and the electric field to which it gives rise, or to Einstein's Principle of Equivalence in the General Theory of Relativity, or the one example we will develop somewhat by way of illustration—Fermat's Principle of Least Time.

In the last example, we imagine a location in space above the smooth surface of a still pond, for example, the end of a willow branch on a windless morning. Imagine further a pebble on the bottom of the pond crisply visible through the clear water. Ask now what path a ray of light will take if it is to travel from the pebble beneath the surface to the tip of the willow branch where, perhaps, it enters our eye. The answer to this question is that the light will travel along a path that will take it from the one spot to the other in the least time. It does not travel straight from the pebble to the branch because light goes more slowly in water than it does in air. Accordingly the light must "shrewdly" gauge how far it should go in water and how far in air so as to minimize the time of travel. What cosmic mystery permits "it" to "know" this in advance? Well, of course it cannot "know" anything in advance. The expression of an optical law in this way points up a mysterious regularity amounting almost to an intentionality in the behavior of the light ray. And, although a deeper study of the same principle will show it to be the result of the statistical behavior of light quanta, this more abstract expression in no way denies the classical description which remains wonderfully mysterious and beautiful. All light rays travelling along all paths, through all combinations of media, whether reflected and refracted or not, behave according to one principle, the principle of taking the path that requires the least time.

We can now summarize our conclusions by saying that the tenacity with which some theoretical understandings are held, even in the face of contradictory evidence, is likely to be grounded in one or more of three kinds of experience, all of which can be understood as limit-experiences.

(1) The experience of disclosure, because of its revelational aspect (something we will later call an ontological flash), carries a conviction, the strength of which surpasses the significance of the empirical data which may have stimulated it.

(2) The concatenation of independent premises which, all taken together, imply a state of affairs that is eventually observed, promotes a limit sense of the presence of truth. This situation can be described as being of the following form: if all these things (A_1, A_2, A_3, . . .) are the case, then B will be the case. However, B *is* the case! Indeed, the more complicated the theoretical structure that forms the basis of the prediction, the stronger will be the sense of the truth of all the premises, which is derived from a confirmation of the conclusion. We accept the truth of the premises in spite of the fact that to accept a premise as true on the basis of an observation of the truth of the conclusion, is invalid logically.

(3) Finally, the experience of beauty, frequently observed as sublime simplicity (in contrast with the foregoing case of extreme complexity) carries its own mystery and seems to harmonize with the very faculties that make human knowing possible. This situation can be described as being of this form: this Z is all that we need to explain these many phenomena (Y_1, Y_2, Y_3, . . .) that are the case.

When we come to know by way of one of these cognitive limit-experiences, what we have come to know can become so much a part of us that it is difficult for any lesser experience to cause us to doubt.

• •

Gerald Holton's distinction between public science and private science (S_2 and S_1, respectively) enables us to show how the "nascent moment" is intrinsic to scientific activity. His distinction also provides a context wherein scientific discovery can be understood to have a religious dimension.

Indeed, the appropriateness of religious terminology is noteworthy. For example, in the description of the experience of "knowing" that something is scientifically true before one has shown that it is true by analysis, we said that this knowledge gives rise to what might be called the tenacity of faith. Here would seem to be an instance of the trust and confidence which persists in scientific investigation through negativities and even against evidence to the contrary. What is so interesting about the experience of the nascent moment and about S_1 in general is that it challenges the usual posture of S_2, which is categorically opposed to faith. William C. Clifford, for example, called faith "overbelief"—the religious tendency to go beyond or to ignore evidence.[20] William James, however, debated Clifford on this issue and held there are many instances in the sphere of intelligent and responsible decision in which humans are called upon to "go beyond" the evidence. In the situation of a drowning child, for example, one has to make a quick decision about the possibility of rescue and act even though one knows that one has never before swum quite that far.

In the sphere of religion, faith is distinguished from but is not unrelated to knowledge. Faith, at the level of experience, may be described as a trust and confidence in one's situation which allows one to live and die with dignity. At the level of understanding, faith is a confidence in knowledge-in-process or in the sudden eruption of new understanding not yet validated or verified. At the level of judgment, faith is an affirmation of the world understood through knowledge-in-process or through a singularly new way of understanding. At the level of decisive action, faith is the enactment of a world of meanings based on one's affirmation of the world as understood.

At the same time as it is related to knowledge, faith is a surpassing of knowledge. That is, when we speak of knowledge we refer usually to those understandings which are communicated through appropriate logic of validation and verified through adequate intersubjective means. Faith is best distinguished from knowledge at the experiential level, the point at which we experience ourselves at the limits of our previous knowledge or at the brink of some new understanding. The experience of faith need not necessarily "precede" understanding, judgment, and decisive action, however. In fact, one can conceive of a decisive action which "opens up" a whole new experience for the self. Speaking historically, John Cobb called attention to the way in which the Christian understanding of faith differs both from the Pharisaic understanding of religion (which, as the Law, is used contrapuntally in the Christian Scriptures) and from the archaic understanding of religion (in which the individual either is a passive instrument of the gods or becomes a manipulator of impersonal spirit-force). Rather, faith is an "indwelling, empowering and transforming personal Spirit interacting with human personal spirit." [21]

With this understanding of the concept of religious faith, Part One, a revisionary analysis of conventional meanings in science and religion, is complete. Chapter one was a critical analysis of two recent developments in science and religion: the turn to language and the use of the concept of myth as an attempt to build a bridge between scientific and religious meanings. In chapter two, however, the common-sense understanding of experience as perception was questioned and some of the premises which follow from this flawed notion were challenged. Distinguishing between immediate and mediated experience, bodies and things, we shifted to the phenomenological model of experience, in which all of the operations of consciousness become explicit. In chapter three, some common-sense understandings of method in science and religion were questioned. In science, we tend to think that we know more than we do and to think that we can do less than we actually can. In religion, we tend to think that subjectivity takes precedence over objectivity. Having made these negative criticisms, in chapter four we came back to discover a common feature to both science and religion: namely, that knowledge-in-process is fundamental to both knowledge and belief in both fields.

We have completed the primarily analytical side of our study in Part One. In Part Two, which is predominantly constructive, we propose a theory of metaphor which will incorporate the nascent moment of understanding and knowledge-in-process in such a way as to provide a new basis for understanding the fundamental similarity and complementary nature of science and religion.

PART 2

NEW UNDERSTANDINGS THROUGH METAPHOR

CHAPTER FIVE

Introduction to Part 2

Until now we have been operating primarily in an analytical mode of thought. We have explored the epistemological premises that underlie the fields of science and religion, and we have reached some agreement regarding the conditions for understanding in either domain.

However, our task is not only to evaluate the ways science and religion have been related in the past nor only to examine the particular assumptions held by scientists and theologians (as well as the populace at large) about what they do.

In this chapter we move into the constructive part of our work.

THE TURN TOWARD EPISTEMOLOGY

The first part of our exploration of the way we come to know our world through science and religion has focused appropriately on the details of human experience, for there can be no knowledge without concomitant experience. However, the emphasis on experience invariably tends to constrict the focus of concern to what individual humans perceive in their present world, at the expense of the developed traditions in science and religion. And so, before developing further our particular perspective on the processing of knowledge in science and religion, we reassess science and religion as fields of meanings.

Modern natural science provides an extraordinarily effective way of knowing the world. Of this there can be no doubt. Furthermore, the great bulk of this knowledge is received knowledge, the fruits of the labors of generations of systematically inquisitive human beings. Newton made more than a statement of

85

polite modesty when he said that he had stood on the shoulders of giants. But it is also true that modern natural science teaches us almost nothing about our artistic and literary cultural heritage. Testimony to this is the fact that one can be an extraordinarily successful scientist without knowing anything about human history including, ironically, the history of science itself. We must conclude, then, that modern science knows a world that is not a whole world. As a model of the way human beings come to know, science is incomplete.

The situation with respect to religion is analogous and complementary. Can there be any doubt of the effectiveness of religious understandings of the world? Even before science developed as a disciplined transmission of knowledge, religious traditions shaped the understandings of generations. Unlike an understanding in natural science, a religious understanding of the world usually provides cognitive space for the dominant cultural artifacts (art, literature, music, architecture) of the world. What a religious understanding fails to provide, however, is information for constructing any particular process or object. We may turn to religion for guidance with respect to human goals but it rarely provides an account of the elements involved in achieving these goals. The faith of Moses may have held back the waters of the Red Sea in order for the Hebrews to pass, but his faith is not expected to provide an explanation of the density or the properties of water which make safe passage through water so precarious. It is here that natural science makes its contribution.

Historical changes in attitudes toward health and the growth of medical knowledge provide a useful example of the complementary aspect of religious and scientific knowledge. Early understandings of human dysfunction involved the exercise of divine power (the story of Job) or the mechanism of possession by spirits (the story of Christ and the lame beggar). In neither case was the desired goal, remedy, or treatment dependent on knowledge of the physiology of the human body. By themselves, healing rites have not been effective means to alleviate human illness and suffering.

Anatomical research, which began in earnest during the Renaissance and culminated in the development of medical science was, in its early stages, seriously hampered by religious beliefs and traditions. In particular, the Christian belief in physical resurrection obstructed the systematic exploration of human physiology for several centuries. Nevertheless, the past 150 years have seen the development of a highly sophisticated medical science that provides the knowledge and understanding necessary to achieve, on a large scale, the alleviation of human suffering, a goal articulated originally on the basis of religious, particularly Christian, understandings.

Today a still larger understanding of the relation of human death to human integrity and happiness recognizes that medical science, precisely because of its formulation as a natural science, is unable to "treat the whole person." We realize that there is more to human health than mere proper physiological functioning. Once again we are being reminded that the scientific view of the world is not, by itself, an adequate view. Human needs, whether medical or epistemological, are only partially met in terms of either natural science or religion taken separately.

Where does that leave us, then, with respect to a human understanding of the world? Can any *Weltanschauung* be adequate if it is constructed from a religious perspective alone or from a natural science perspective alone? Given the vastness of the traditions of knowledge and the distinctions in the issues that science and religion claim to address, either perspective taken alone must necessarily be incomplete. Hence the perceived need for reconciliation.

Linguistic analysts believe, with considerable justification as we have already observed, that they have achieved this reconciliation. However, their reliance on the similarity of linguistic forms in the expression of religious and scientific beliefs, we have argued, is inadequate. Linguistic expressions of belief and statements of truth are now properly understood not to be the hard, stable, and unyielding objects they were once thought to be. They are understood today to be objects that change and move with the speaker or the hearer, with the writer or the reader.

Without this review, the theory of metaphor which follows in chapter six might seem merely another analysis of an important linguistic form. Unless we show at the outset that an emphasis on process epistemology, on knowlege-in-process, is fundamentally different from the analysis of linguistic statements, we are in danger of being misunderstood. How, then, does a form of linguistic expression such as metaphor contribute to a process epistemology rather than to a more traditional analysis?

The crucial difference comes in the rejection of statements, religious or scientific, as the only appropriate objects of study. Instead we look at the processes of different kinds of expression, including linguistic expression, as models of processes of thought. Even if metaphor is conceived of as a merely rhetorical device, it is clear that its use causes people to change the way they think about something. An understanding of the way such changes take place provides a basis for understanding the way that new knowledge comes into existence. Here the processes in science and in religion are the same. We seek, then, to take advantage of the fact that warrants for belief can be found in the processes that culminate in belief and that, at this level, science and religion are equally valid and have comparable claims on the loyalty of intellect.

At the same time, we seek to correct the simplistic view of science as a unified body of accepted meanings and of religion as a hopelessly fragmented body of diverse doctrines. This mistaken view stems from a too-particularistic understanding of the elements of science and of religion. In this view, the meanings of science are confined to particular theories, for example, of movement, energy, or light. The meanings of religion are taken to be particular doctrines, for example, of God, creation, life-after-death. Often the meanings of religion are further fractionalized into particular traditional symbols and objects, such as the cross, the Buddha, the Covenant, or the Torah. This kind of particularism is the basis for the belief that the history of science is uniform and uncontested whereas the histories of religions are irremediably diversified and discontinuous with one another. As a result, claims in science are seen as unqualifiedly universalistic while claims in religion are denied any objective status.

The truth lies somewhere between these two extremes. We wish to break out of the particularistic view of the elements of science and religion and instead conceive of them as complementary at the same level and kind of generalization. We do this by the introduction of the notion of "themata."

THEMATIC ORIGINS OF SCIENTIFIC THOUGHT

Gerald Holton coined the phrase "thematic origins of scientific thought" to make a distinction between public science and private science. His understanding of the way scientific thought develops on the bases of recurrent cognitive structures he calls "themata" is particularly helpful:

> . . . the significance . . . of themata is indicated by the fact that they force upon people notions that are usually regarded as paradoxical, ridiculous, or outrageous. I am thinking here of the "absurdities" of Copernicus's moving earth, Bruno's infinite worlds, Galileo's inertial motion of bodies in a horizontal plane, Newton's gravitational action without a palpable medium of communication, Darwin's descent of man from lower creatures, Einstein's twin paradox and maximum speed for signals, Freud's conception of sexuality of children, or Heisenberg's indeterminacy conception. The wide interest and intensity of such debates, among both scientists and enraged or intrigued laymen, is an indication of the strength with which themata—and frequently conflicting ones—are always active in our consciousness.[1]

Themata, it would seem, force us to examine the underlying continuities between seemingly disparate concepts.

In Holton's view, a relatively short list of themata provides the underlying structure for all of our theoretical constructions, ancient as well as modern. Holton differs from Kuhn in that the latter emphasized discontinuity and revolution while Holton opted for an emphasis on a more or less cyclical loss and reemergence. "For contrary to the physical theories . . . themata are not proved or disproved. Rather they rise and fall and rise again with the tides of contemporary usefulness."[2]

The idea of the atom provides a good example. At the heart of the concept is elementism, the idea that further subdivision is either impossible or yields merely less of the same. This concept also leads, paradoxically, to the concept of the continuum, the antithesis of atomicity. We move, from the time of the Greeks to the present, through a sequence of elemental concepts usually expressed in atomic form. The Greek elements of earth, air, fire, and water later became the chemical elements which carried their properties down to the level of the chemical atom as the smallest unit. Early atomic theory developed the atom as composed of smaller "atomic" units of electrons, protons and neutrons. These, in turn, become complexes of still more "elementary" particles. In the meantime, alternating contrapuntally like a sixteenth-century fugue, the related but antithetical thema of the continuum or the field comes and goes. Einstein, the inventor of the light particle, or quantum, could not bring himself to believe that theory of the atom explained the fundamental character of the universe. He spent the last third of his life in an apparently fruitless attempt to revive the field as dominant over atomicity, continuity rather than discontinuity as the nature of the universe. If we agree with Holton, as we do, that the development of science is less a matter of the sudden emergence of a truly new concept than it is the rebirth of an old one sometimes in disguise, then it follows that the development of understanding is a matter not of the formation of new themata but of the reformation of old ones. And it is this process of reformation for which we need a model.

THE THEMATA OF RELIGION

In both science and religion, themata constitute the major cognitive structures of epistemological significance. In our conception of science and religion as fields of meanings, we shall expect to find that a thema, such as vitalism in science or theism in religion, will be variously expressed within a particular tradition of science or religion. Within either religion or science understood cross-culturally, themata that are affirmed and rejected appear, disappear, and reappear in a variety of motifs. Invariably, however, the cognitive structures of major meanings and is-sues—of themata—remain.

What are some of the themata of religion? To begin with, obviously they are what have been called the traditional doc-trines: God, grace, sin. Stated more philosophically, for example by Kant, they are God, freedom, immortality, or more contempo-rarily, the sacred, world, humankind. These three themata, vari-ously expressed, are a representative but not exhaustive list.

What does it mean to identify these themata? On one level, it signifies that these are the major "things" (Lonergan's sense of objects as related to one another) of religion. On another, it re-flects an historical knowledge-in-process—a history of question-ing, of multiple forms of understanding, of affirmations and deni-als informed structurally by these themata. What is often lost sight of in comparative, as distinct from epistemological, studies is that all of the forms of theistic, atheistic or agnostic expres-sion—God as shephard, God as illusion, God as judge, God as consolation, God as fellow-companion, God as threat, God as lure, God as love—participate in the structure of "things" which give rise to the themata of God. God, therefore, is one of those central themata which persists; it may disappear or re-emerge, but it endures in one form or another.

What is the advantage of treating the "things" of religion and science as "themata"? First of all, we avoid the hypostatization that has occurred within each field of meanings with the use of other terms. It is not sufficient to extend the use of terms em-ployed at present in each field to the other. For example, it is true that doctrines (originally a religious term) occur in both science and religion, but the term is unfortunately aligned in sci-ence with dogmatic positions or essentialist categories. And hy-potheses (a term widely used in science) "exist" in both religious and scientific understanding, but the implication of mere tenta-tiveness haplessly disengages the term hypothesis from the realm of true probabilities in religion.

Second, we wish to by-pass any reification of "things" in both science and religion by focusing on the disciplines as fields of meanings rather than as repositories of truths. In this sense, we focus on the relations among "things" as distinct from things-in-themselves. What clusters of issues, for example, give rise to the themata "God"? One set of issues has to do with the relation of human beings to history—the sense that humans have of time, its extension and limitations. Questions pertaining to beginnings and end-times and the possibility of radical societal change constitute the issue of the transcendent and culminate in the notion of a God-of-the-future and of history.

Another set of issues arises out of the phenomenon of inter-subjectivity. Do humans have a spirit which both inheres in and surpasses individual spirit? Why ought one to keep promises in any ultimate sense? What kinds of possible relationships between the spirits of the dead and of the living, as well as among the living, constitute the issue of the personal and give rise to paradigms of inter-relatedness, such as the sacred pantheon, the trinity, the communion of saints, or the hope of the oppressed?

A third set of issues stems from the problem of identity. What does it mean to be a self? a people? a nation? The phenomenon of belonging to a tradition, of expecting subsistence from world and society, constitutes the issue of embodiedness and culminates in the notion of God as providential and immanent in the human situation. Still another set of issues is centered in the human activity of knowing. Questions arise: What are the possibilities and fruits of belief? What are the roles of doubting? of wagering? of understanding? of questioning? This set of issues resides in the notion of God as limit-question.

Themata, then, are the "things" of science and religion. And because they are so readily, even if controvertibly, identified, they are responsible in large measure for the stability of science and religion in spite of, or perhaps because of, all the changes that have come about over the years.

It may seem as though the fluctuations of meanings could be held in abeyance while we describe the basic elements of the two disciplines. But now the changes in the themata, as well as the stability, must be accounted for. The changes are the result of a process (coming-to-know) closely related to language but not explicated merely in linguistic form. In chapter six the metaphoric process is introduced as an explanation of how new knowledge comes into existence. Only one task remains for this chapter: to distinguish our use of metaphor as related to fields of meanings, or themata, from the use of metaphor by the theorists discussed in chapter one.

THE FIELD OF MEANINGS

If we are to distinguish between linguistic form and episte-mological process, we must refine our understanding of the relationship between language and meaning. Epistemological development is more a processing of meanings than it is a processing of words.

If one person utters a word that puzzles another, the latter is likely to ask, "What does that mean?" Replies to such a query normally fall into two categories, the synonym and the definition. Whichever reply is chosen the question can be repeated so as to elicit a new response. After several such responses have been made there emerges a "context" which comprises the relations among the elements that made up the set of responses. It is this configuration of relations, understood as a context, that we call the meaning of the utterance. Such a configuration of relations is part of a larger fabric of relations, a network that makes it possible to open a dictionary, look up a word, choose a synonym of that word, look up the synonym, choose a synonym of that synonym, look it up, etc. Often the sequence will close upon itself and we are returned to the original word. Sometimes the sequence leads us far afield to the point where we are no longer able to see the relation between a word presently under examination and the word with which we started. In either case we call the conceptual region traversed in the process a "field of meanings."

How does this conception of meaning, as exemplified in the system of language, relate to knowledge-in-process? Since the development and expression of new knowledge does not necessarily require an increase in vocabulary, we can presume that increased knowledge relates in a fundamental way to changes that take place in the relations that exist among words, that is, to changes in our "field of meanings."

This conception of meaning suggests a further dimension to Holton's themata. The fabric of relations mentioned above can be understood to contain thematic elements rather like the elements that go together to make up a pattern in an oriental rug. In the next chapter we will make the relationship of themata to the field of meanings explicit by showing a thematic concept as a curved path that traverses a field of meanings.

Those who pursue a linguistic approach to an analysis of science and religion may agree with our present formulation of meaning as residing in the relational "space" between words rather than in the words themselves. But their further analysis differs from ours in that their focus on specific statements in science and religion, even metaphorical ones, precludes the emphasis on process and change that we find so necessary. For example, polysemy (i.e., multiple meanings of a given word) may create ambiguity in a linguistic analysis, but it does not generate change. Metaphor itself, if dealt with only in terms of particular verbal metaphors, becomes merely an example of a final product. Our analysis differs by centering instead on the process of making metaphors. For this analysis the quasi-spatial concept we have called a field of meanings will be employed.

Fields of meanings can now be generalized to include sets of cognitive relations of many different kinds, not merely those that arise in verbal language. In mathematics, for example, we find a different kind of "language" which deals in a formal way with relations and provides fields of meanings that are distinct from those of verbal language. More generally we find in music or the visual arts additional examples of relations between elements that comprise still other fields of meanings. It will be important to bear in mind that, although many of our examples are also members of verbal language fields, the conclusions we draw in terms of the role played by metaphor apply to those more general fields of meanings as well.

CHAPTER SIX

A Theory of Metaphor

"ALL THE WORLD's a stage and all the men and women merely players. They have their exits and their entrances; and one man in his time plays many parts. . . ." This familiar passage from Shakespeare's *As You Like It* is a good example of a literary metaphor of the kind which has traditionally dominated the entire discussion of metaphor. Metaphor for us, however, is more than a linguistic artifact. It is a structural change in a field of meanings.

THE LIMITS OF METAPHOR

In order to recognize the need for a theory of metaphor, let us recall Gerald Holton's distinction between S_1 and S_2, that is, between private science as the personal struggle of the scientist and public science as a contingent plane of well-formulated meaning.[1] Holton's concern in making the distinction was to broaden our understanding of what scientific thought involves. He argued that what is ordinarily meant by science is S_2, public science, and that, however difficult, it is important though difficult to understand the role of S_1, the arena of the scientist's imaginative processes.

To this end, Holton constructed a way of forcing us to think about S_1 and S_2 together. He introduced the term "thematic" to emphasize the non-deterministic dimension of scientific theory and to call our attention to the multiple factors in S_1 which lead to S_2. These factors, he said, must include the emotional, aesthetic, and social forces intrinsic to scientific inquiry. Nevertheless, the effect of Holton's constructive analysis is to increase our understanding of what goes into S_2. His analysis does not contribute especially to our understanding of S_1, the day-to-day struggle with scientific understanding, because he left S_1 largely to the vagaries of the individual scientist.

The same problem exists correlatively in religion although the need for conceptual structures for understanding R_1 (the arena of the theologian's imaginative processes) may appear to be less urgent since many words relating to R_1, for example, revelation, inspiration, and conversion, are in common usage. But the point to be made pertains to both science and religion: unless we have a concept to sustain our understanding of the "nascent" moments of religion and science, S_1 and R_1 are too easily left in the realm of the private and perhaps even of the occult. The task before us, then, is to design a concept to express our understandings of S_1 and R_1 which will later enable us to relate them to S_2 and R_2, and subsequently S_1 and S_2 to R_1 and R_2. Holton's notion of "thematic," while helpful toward establishing a necessary continuity between S_1 and S_2 (and by appropriation R_1 and R_2), leaves for us the task of understanding S_1 and R_1, the "nascent" moments in science and religion. We need, in other words, a theory which will better explicate what happens in S_1 and R_1. In our efforts to understand these nascent moments, we turn to theories of metaphor.

Some attempts in this direction have already been made. In his *Metaphor and Myth in Science and Religion* (1976), for example, Earl MacCormac stated his own view of the appropriateness of metaphor for understanding science and religion.

> Without the language of metaphor neither science nor religion could flourish. Both disciplines are "metaphoric" in the sense that they are erected upon the foundations of root-metaphors. Such hypotheses about the nature of the world and human experience are epiphoric in that they were conceived of by analogy to the personal knowledge of the inventor. They are also diaphoric in that they suggest ways of viewing things that are not literally true. But, science and religion are "metaphoric" in another sense as well. Each enterprise utilizes individual metaphors to convey ideas about the unknown.[2]

Now we are in basic agreement with MacCormac and others who point out the use of metaphor in science and religion. Yet we have difficulties with their understanding of metaphor. Often it is not clear just what the notion of metaphor includes and excludes. On the one hand, for example, metaphor is equated with new meaning; metaphors, that is, "offer new ways of understanding which we can test in experiments or in our experiences." On the other hand, metaphor is taken to include established meanings as well; "they suggest ways of viewing things that are not literally true." Each of the two senses of metaphor, for MacCormac, have epiphoric and diaphoric aspects: "they must be accessible by analogy to what we have already perceived and known" and "they offer new ways of understanding which we can test in experiment or in our experience." But it is doubtful to our minds that the term metaphor can be employed advantageously to signify all of those senses at once—doubtful, too, that all of these senses constitute a coherent concept of metaphor.

Metaphor has been understood in a number of ways, but certain consistencies appear as one reviews the major theories of metaphor. Among the Greeks, with whom we first encounter the notion of metaphor in the Western tradition, Plato is first even though he never formulated a theory of metaphor as such. He is important also because Aristotle's theory, which shaped many of the subsequent Western understandings of metaphor, was designed with Plato's objections in mind.

Plato was opposed to rhetoric of all kinds. In the dialogue *Gorgias* (c. 400 B.C.E.), this opposition becomes the basis for his views on art, and by implication, metaphor as well.[3] Plato regarded rhetoric as dangerous: he said that, like the use of cosmetics, rhetoric is an act of deception. Poets are among the worst offenders since they engage in dissimulation. Although he does not banish all poets from his ideal state, Plato nevertheless suggested in *The Republic* (c. 370 B.C.E.) that any poet who dares to visit the republic should be escorted to the border. Much of Plato's opposition to artists and poets seems to have stemmed from his ambition to formulate a new way of seeking knowledge by means of philosophical reflection over and against mere opinion. Regardless, his negative view of metaphor as deception set the scene for Aristotle's positive evaluation of metaphor as the ingenious perception of likenesses.

From the beginning, we depart radically from the Platonic lack of understanding of metaphor, as well as from his derogatory attitude toward the uses of metaphor. Rather than being a cosmetic for purposes of deceit, metaphor is for us a process of creating new meaning.

Aristotle's views have been the basis for virtually all Western thought about metaphor—often repeated, sometimes elaborated upon, seldom disputed. Aristotle placed metaphor in both the fields of rhetoric (thus relating it closely to the art of persuasion) and of philosophical argumentation (thus relating it closely to the logic of probability).[4] Although his references to metaphor are largely scattered in the *Rhetoric* and the *Poetics* (c. 320 B.C.E.), his central achievement for the cause of metaphor is clear. By giving metaphor a basis in philosophy as well as in rhetoric, he made truth as well as persuasion its goal and restored to metaphor a positive function.

Aristotle took metaphor to be a sign of genius. He did not think that the making of metaphors could be learned from others since it involves an intuitive perception of the similarities in dissimilarities. In his view, metaphor surpasses other forms of expression because of its ability to attract attention and to transmit maximum information most efficiently. He proposed that comparison and analogy be understood as forms of metaphor rather than vice versa.

Aristotle's treatment of metaphor can be summarized as follows: (1) As something which happens to the noun, metaphor is attached to the word rather than to discourse in general. (2) As something that displaces meaning away from or toward another meaning, metaphor always borrows from another field of meanings. (3) As something that is strange or rare by comparison with current meanings, metaphor incurs some sense of distance from ordinary language. (4) As meaning which moves from genre to species, from species to genre, or from species to species, metaphor plays across several typologies and even threatens to displace some elements within them.

Aristotle's theory allows the process of metaphor-making to come to the fore, especially in the *Poetics* where metaphor can be seen to be related to plot or dramatic action. Our theory of metaphor, as developed in the following chapters, does not so much contradict Aristotle's theory as develop, amplify, and extend it in new ways. We clarify the relationship between analogy and metaphor, modify the understanding of metaphor so that it pertains to non-linguistic as well as linguistic meaning, and free metaphor from its confinement to literary contexts. These are the issues most in need of clarification and resolution today.

After Aristotle, the understanding of metaphor degenerated by losing its relation to philosophy. For example, Quintilian, a Roman rhetorician, in his book *Institutio Oratoria* (c. 96 C.E.) on the training of an orator from childhood through maturity, treated metaphor as a trope. For him, metaphor was essentially a substitute expression to be used by the orator whenever propriety allowed. He did not regard metaphor as the most excellent form of expression (as did Aristotle) but rather as an abbreviated comparison. Quintilian assumed that meaning is literal and that the rhetorician substitutes other terms in order to achieve more persuasive speech. His explanation of the role of metaphor expanded upon the dimensions of Aristotle's many-faceted theory. Quintilian listed four classes of metaphor:

> In the first we substitute one living thing for another, as in the passage where the poet, speaking of a charioteer, says, "The steersman then/ With mighty effort wrenched his charger found," or when Livy says that Scipio was continually barked at by Cato. Secondly, inanimate things may be substituted for inanimate, as in the Virgilian, "And gave his fleet the rein," or inanimate may be substituted for animate, as in "Did the Argive bulwark fall by sword of Fate?", or animate for inanimate, as in the following lines: "The shepherd sits unknowing on the height/ Listening the roar from some far mountain brow." [5]

Quintilian's theory of metaphor has as its focus the manipulation of nouns; ours is concerned with the manipulation of meanings.

Metaphor continued to be cut off from philosophy in medieval exegesis and rhetoric. Demonstrating how little the understanding of metaphor had changed in almost two centuries, we find Pierre Fontanier (1830) treating metaphor as ornament to the plain statement of thought.[6] Fontanier's thought was the logical outcome of Quintilian's theory. In Fontanier's theory, metaphor is merely one of many figures of speech; it does not provide any new information. Since all figures are improper terms, the reader's task, according to Fontanier, is to find the proper term. Paraphrase, in other words, is everything. Metaphor here is a mere accident in naming. Here, also, rhetoric is merely the act of pleasing (as distinct from persuading). Metaphor has altogether lost its link with philosophical argument and concomitantly, its relation to truth and reality.

Georg Wilhelm Friedrich Hegel, writing about the same time as Fontanier, regarded metaphor with ambivalence. Although Hegel appeared to have been fascinated by the metaphors he found in literary texts, he never got beyond the view that metaphor is a primitive form needing to be surpassed in other, more developed forms of expression. Most words, he said in his *Vorlesungen über die Aesthetik* (lectures given at intervals between 1813 and 1831), are "independently intelligible" expressions; metaphors are not. Metaphors do lend vivacity to poetic expression, but at the same time they can quite as easily make the whole passage "unwieldy, overloading it thus with its emphasis on singular aspects."[7]

Hegel, on the whole, regarded metaphor as offering support to "imaginative vision in the direction of clear definition." Metaphor can "bring home the sense" of an indefinite word by means of an image. The genius of metaphor, for him, was not its own excellence as contrasted with other forms of expression as it was for Aristotle, but its psychological potency: to respond "to a need and . . . [to] the emotional life." The "need" to which Hegel referred is that of the dialectic from the simple and obvious into something hidden under the "attraction which distinction offers." Indeed, at base, metaphor for Hegel, was a distraction:

> The metaphor, in fact, is always an interruption of the logical course of conception and invariably to that extent a distraction, because it starts images and brings them together, which are not immediately connected with the subject and its significance, and for this reason tends to . . . divert the

attention from the same to matter cognate with themselves, but strange to both.[8]

Bound essentially by an evolutionary view of language, Hegel never developed a theory of metaphor that matched his use of it. In the end, he replaced it with other cognitive forms.

Quintilian, Fontanier, and Hegel, representative of the major approaches to metaphor from Aristotle to the nineteenth century, all understood metaphor as the substitution of one noun for another. With I. A. Richards, metaphor began to be understood as the interaction of one word or phrase with another, involving tension of meaning and precluding substitution of accepted meanings as a resolution of the tension. In Richards, furthermore, we find the beginning of the contemporary shift away from metaphor as a classification device to metaphor as a principle of generating meaning. In his *Philosophy of Rhetoric* (1936), Richards criticized previous literary critical assumptions that metaphor is only embellishment or beauty added to plain meaning (which alone really matters), something that "regardless of the figures" can be gathered by the patient reader. In his theory, metaphor is understood as an interaction between the tenor (sense) or expression and its vehicle (figure or archetypal image).[9] For Richards, metaphor was no longer a particular kind of word. Indeed, he thought a word might be both literal and metaphoric at the same time: it might support many different metaphors, or it might serve to focus many different meanings into one meaning.

Although Richards was not especially clear on the outcome of the dynamic process of metaphor, he was sure that it was not merely a matter of comparison. To interpret a metaphor was not an etymological exercise; for him, it was an issue of how we take the words. Without analyzing in depth the effect that is produced by metaphor (although the examples he provided demonstrate that there is the effect he claimed), Richards noted that a metaphor sets up a tension between tenor and vehicle, a tension that is greater in proportion to the remoteness of the things presented as tenor and vehicle.

Richards' was the first theory since Aristotle's to do justice to the power and complexity of metaphor. In contrast to our own

interest in how metaphors work, however, Richards was ultimately interested in how different persons understand metaphor.
In this sense, his emphasis was more on the psychological implications of metaphor.

One of the more explicit attempts to further the epistemological character of metaphor is found in the work of Susanne Langer. Langer's general intention was to extend Kant's critique of
reason to other forms of understanding. Her work on metaphor
in *Philosophy in a New Key* (1942) was done from an epistemological perspective and in that sense is close to our own. However,
whereas she regarded epistemology as "all that is left of a worn-
out philosophical heritage" and symbol as the cue for a new philosophical theme, we return to the metaphoric process and its relationships with other cognitive processes, specifically those in
science and religion.

Langer perceived the power of metaphor in the ability of language, even with a small vocabulary, to "embrace a multimillion
things." Metaphor is the principle by which new words are born.
Langer was alone among the theorists to notice that metaphor is
the "elementary mode in which our first adventures in conscious
abstraction occur." Metaphor, that is, gives evidence of "abstrac-
tive seeing":

> One might say that . . . metaphor is the law of [the] life [of
> language]. It is the force that makes it essentially *relational*,
> intellectual, forever showing up new, abstractable *forms* in
> reality, forever laying down a deposit of old, abstracted con-
> cepts in an increasing treasure of general words.[10]

Langer's theory is closely bound up with the evolution of
speech, in particular with its function of giving something a
name. Literal language for her is the "repository of language."
While Langer argued persuasively for the need to broaden the
philosophy of meaning to include metaphor as new meaning, it
was not her ambition, as it is ours, to attempt to provide a theory
of that process.

In *The Burning Fountain* (1954), Philip Wheelwright was interested in the relationship between metaphor and reality and in
the function of metaphor in religion. He argued for two funda-

mentally different forms of language—the literal and the metaphorical. The former he said is suited to ordinary and scientific
truths, the latter to non-empirical and intuitive truth. Scientific
language is either epiphoric (immediately assimilative) or diaphoric (mediately constructive). Metaphor, according to Wheelwright, is the tension between epiphor and diaphor. As language
that is "alive," "fluid," "vital," "full," "plurisignative," "open,"
"affective," and "resonant," metaphor has an indisputably ontological character.[11]

Although Wheelwright's major contribution was his vivid description of metaphor and his demonstration that metaphor re-
capitulates ontology, the effect of his theory was to dichotomize
science and religion. His proposal of a double-language theory,
in which the languages of science and religion are autonomous
and irreducible one to the other, had the effect of closing off
further discourse on their relationship. In place of a double-
language theory, we assume that all language is both potentially
univocal and potentially plurisignative. On this basis, it is not
accurate or useful to differentiate science and religion exclusively
in terms of where the emphasis on their use of language lies.
Nevertheless, Wheelwright's description of plurisignative language was especially helpful for reversing the trend toward
positivism in linguistic analysis in the 1940's.

To understand the philosophical as well as the literary implications of metaphor in a positive sense was Max Black's intention.
In his *Models and Metaphors: Studies in Language and Philosophy*
(1962), Black made a systematic summary of theories of metaphor, dividing them into substitution views of metaphor, comparison views (which he treated as a sub-set of substitution
views), and interaction views. In his understanding of the interaction view of metaphor, Black relied heavily upon Richards'
theory in which two different expressions act together to result in
another meaning. Although he finally did not explicate the significance of metaphor for philosophy, Black did assert the non-
translatability of interactive metaphors:

Up to a point, we may succeed in stating a number of the
relevant relations between the two [elements of a meta-

phor]. . . . But the set of literal statements so obtained will not have the same power to inform and enlighten as the original. . . . The loss in such cases is a loss in cognitive content; the relevant weakness of the literal paraphrase is not that it may be tiresomely prolix or boringly explicit . . .; it fails to be a translation because it fails to give the insight that the metaphor did.[12]

Black concluded that only metaphors of interaction are of importance in philosophy since the other two kinds can be replaced with literal translations.

For Black, metaphor is a filter, or a frame, which links a system of associated meanings to a principal subject, its focus. Although he attributed to metaphor the power to shift or to extend meaning, he did not try to account, as we do, for how such changes occur. Black concluded that metaphors are dangerous, yet he thought that to prohibit their use would be an even more dangerous restriction of inquiry.

Mary Hesse's *Models and Analogies in Science* (1966), was one of the first contemporary studies to extend the notion of metaphor to scientific understanding. She proposed to supplement the hypothetico-deductive model of scientific explanation with a metaphoric redescriptive model of explanation developed from Black's theory of metaphor. For Hesse, metaphor was the transfer of a word or words normally held within a secondary system, to language describing a primary system. As an example, Hesse discussed the statement, "Sound is propagated by wave motion." Here sound (the primary system) is the *explanandum*, describable in observation language, and the remainder of the statement (taken from a secondary system) is described either in observation language or in the language of familiar theory.[13]

In the final analysis, Hesse's metaphor is really what we will refer to as analogy: that is, she regarded the explanatory function as intrinsic to the scientific metaphor rather than as resulting from it. In addition, we find Hesse's theory to be confined to language in spite of her attempt to address the question of metaphor in science. We shall attempt to lift that restriction in our own theory.

One of the most prolific theorists of metaphor, Paul Ricoeur, understood metaphor as praxis, that is, as generating possible new worlds and new ways of orienting oneself in them. In his book on metaphor, *La Métaphore vive* (1975), Ricoeur drew upon the traditions of literary criticism, philosophy, theology, and linguistic analysis. According to Ricoeur, the function of metaphor is that of presenting "in an *open* fashion, by means of a conflict *between* identity and difference, the process that, in a *covert* manner, generates semantic grids by fusion of differences *into* identity."[14] Ricoeur carried his treatment of metaphor forward from the rhetorical to the semantic and the hermeneutic. Corresponding to each of these contexts he systematically arranged the common views of metaphor, several of which we have seen in previous theorists: metaphor as word, metaphor as phrase, metaphor as work or discourse. Ricoeur's argument, most simply stated, was that the metaphoric function of language impels human discourse not only toward new meanings but toward an appropriate philosophical language to understand them.

In his view, metaphor constitutes two energies in human discourse. At the origin of the metaphoric process is a "gravitational" energy. Ricoeur called this the "ontological vehemence" of the metaphor in that it embodies a "semantic aim."[15] But because the ontological vehemence is only an indication of meaning and neither its determination nor its specification, it generates a second energy—philosophical disclosure—which proceeds from the very structures of spirit which philosophy has as its task to articulate. The meaning of a metaphor, said Ricoeur, is not "drawn" from anywhere. It is a momentous creation of language, a semantic innovation which has no status in established language, either as designation or as connotation.

Ricoeur's theory of metaphor has been helpful in the construction of our own, particularly the sense in which he understood metaphor as emergent meaning. However, Ricoeur was interested primarily in linguistic metaphors. For example, in *Interpretation Theory: Discourse and the Surplus of Meaning* he used metaphor, which he described as a primarily linguistic phenomenon, to disclose the linguistic aspect of symbol.[16] In a later essay, "The Metaphoric Process as Cognition, Imagination, and Feeling," he explored the constitutive function of images and feelings in semantic theories of metaphor.[17] We regard his work as essentially complementary to our own. In our attempt to disclose the non-linguistic character of the metaphoric process, however, we examine pre- and extra-linguistic appearances of metaphor as well.

Another theorist, Samuel Levin, in *The Semantics of Metaphor* (1977), explicitly confined his study of metaphor to the field of linguistics and took as his starting point the disparity between those linguists who understood language to be sentences abstracted from speakers and setting and those who understood it also to comprise the knowledge that native speakers have about those sentences. Levin himself understood metaphor to be an instance of semantic deviance and examined the problem from the perspectives of both the analyst and the native speaker. However, he questioned the whole notion of semantic deviance from within linguistics, which regarded metaphor as deviant from the rules of ordinary grammar. His major contribution, however, was the construction of linguistic rules to interpret metaphor. Although his study was more restricted than our own, Levin's treatment of metaphor illustrated how attention to metaphor could bring about a radical change in the way a field of inquiry—in this case linguistic analysis—understands itself.[18]

Among modern theologians who recognized the importance of metaphor—theologians such as William Beardslee, Sallie Mc-Fague, Amos Wilder, Frederick Ferré, Robert Funk, F. W. Dillistone, and Nicholas Lash[19]—David Tracy combined the notion of "limit" and metaphor in a way that is particularly useful for religious understanding. In *Blessed Rage for Order* (1974), Tracy distinguished "common everyday language," in which the primary referents are capable of being indicated without remainder, from "limit-language" in which language refers to something through and beyond the primary referent:

> Reflection upon limit-questions and limit-situations does disclose the reality of a dimension to our lives other than the more usual dimensions: a dimension whose first key is its reality as limit-to our other everyday, moral, scientific, cul-

tural, and political activities; a dimension which . . . discloses a reality, however named and in whatever manner experienced, which functions as a final, now gracious, now frightening, now trustworthy, now absurd, always uncontrollable limit-of the very meaning of existence itself.[20]

Limit-language, for Tracy, includes myth, symbol, metaphor and some kinds of metaphysical language, especially that of analogy.

Specifically on metaphor, Tracy held that all major religions are based upon certain root-metaphors. He employed Ricoeur's theory of metaphor to show the means by which theology can be faithful to the metaphorical language of religious texts. His focus was on the principal traditional metaphors for specific religious traditions, metaphors which demand some kind of correlation with the stated understandings of contemporary experience and language.

Our purpose is to develop an epistemological understanding of metaphor that builds on the foregoing theories yet goes beyond them and, by means of this new understanding of metaphor, to establish that contemporary science and religion share significant epistemological and ontological concerns. Since we will focus on those activities in both religion and science which are metaphoric in the sense of impelling thought toward new meaning, we will not include anything prior to the instance of the disclosure of new meaning, nor will we account for the possible metaphoric origin of all language, a genetic problem all of its own. By studying the way in which the metaphoric process generates new meaning, we demonstrate the epistemological function—that is, the special role among all the other ways of knowing—played by metaphor.

• •

It is becoming increasingly clear that the focus of our analysis must be on the human activity of coming-to-know, on knowledge-in-process, on that process which must necessarily take place within the realm of what Holton has called S_1 and to which we have related a corresponding realm R_1. It is here, in the creation of scientific or religious knowledge, that the commonness of human enterprises is manifest. The focus on how scientists and theologians "create" meanings requires that we attempt to construct a model that elucidates the way in which they came to know what they claim to know.

For this reason we must go further than those theorists for whom the emphasis is on communication, on language, on the way in which knowledge is sustained, and the role that metaphor plays in that process. For most theorists, metaphor is expressive and descriptive rather than inventive and constructive. For us, the emphasis is on the role that metaphor plays in the process of knowledge coming into existence. Our concern is not with the explanation of an idea but with the invention of that idea.

In the epistemological process itself, metaphor is understood better as a device of thought than as a device of language. The relation between language and thought is a problem as old as the idea of metaphor itself. From the Platonic assertion that thought is dialogue with the soul to Noam Chomsky's suggestion that thought arises out of an innate generative grammar, we have an implied equivalence of thinking and speaking. Without language there can be no thought.

However, there are modern philosophers who hold, as we do, that there is much that we know but cannot express in language, much that we are unable to communicate. We can think about that which we know but cannot express, for if we could not think about it, we could not be said to know it at all. It follows that we can have thoughts that we cannot express in words, i.e., that thought and language are not equivalent.

Expression in language, then, follows thought and so we must push the metaphoric act back closer to the origins of understanding than to linguistic enactments of metaphor. If metaphor is to be an act of thought we must relate metaphor not to words but to meanings, which brings us, in a curious way, close to Hanson with respect to the act of thinking or observing.

When we say, with Hanson, that observation is theory-laden, we mean to imply that there is far more to what is meant by "theory" than is contained in any particular lingistic expression of a theory. Furthermore, we go farther than Hanson and raise the question of the origin of theories that mediate observations. Ob-

servation itself gives rise to theory through a cognitive process
we call metaphoric. Two assertions taken together can be seen to
constitute an epistemological circle with the metaphoric act as the
driving mechanism. Our next move will be to explicate a theory of
metaphor which we believe will provide this mechanism.

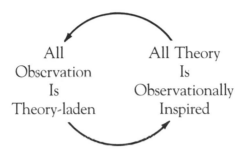

All   All Theory
Observation   Is
Is   Observationally
Theory-laden   Inspired

Fig. 6.1 An epistemological circle.

TOPOLOGIES OF WORLDS OF MEANINGS

In what follows the idea of the world of meanings, introduced
in chapter four, will be expanded so that it can be applied to the
problem of the explication of the idea of analogy, the idea of
metaphor, and then the relationship between them. A model will
show the way in which a world of meanings can be changed,
and, since a model is an analogical device, an analogy will be
used to explain what analogy is. This may seem circular, but it is
often possible to work with an idea given only an ambiguous definition of what that idea is. Since learning proceeds analogically,
we must use analogy in coming to know both analogy and
metaphor.

Let us represent a world of meanings as a flat region of space
and consider this world of meanings as a map of all that we know,
including both the facts of our knowledge as well as the relationships (many and various) between those facts. This map of the
world of meanings can be thought of further as being subdivided
rather naturally into sub-regions that, like continents, are somewhat isolated from each other. These continents of meanings
we will call fields of meanings in the sense that a particular

piece of discourse or argument can be expected to wander through a particular region (field) of the world of meanings without crossing the borders. If, in the course of a conversation, someone introduces elements of another field of meanings we might say that the subject has been changed. On the other hand, if elements from another field of meanings have been introduced in order to explicate an understanding in the original field we might say that the person has created an analogy. This idea of analogy can be expressed in terms of something that happens on our map of the world of meanings.

Assume that within one field of meanings we are confident that our understanding is adequate for our purposes. Think of this understanding as a line or a "road" on our map, a road that we know well. This road traces a curve as it winds from one place to another touching many places in between. If we know this road and most of the places through which it passes and the countryside on both sides of it, we can say that this is familiar territory and that we understand this road. Now imagine that there are two places in another country, another field of meanings, where we do not know the road from one place to the other. We can say that we do not "understand" this area. If the relationship between the two new places were such that we could "transfer" our curving road from the known country to the unknown country so that we could now get from the one new place to the other, we could be said to have created an analogy. Think of analogy as the tracing of a curve by a device such as a pantograph which reproduces a curve, enlarged or reduced, at another location. Such a curve can be understood to represent a thematic concept such as that described by Holton. The relationship as it would appear on a map of the world of meanings might look something like that depicted in Fig. 6.2.

Several aspects of this situation should be noticed. First, it should be apparent that new meaning is created by this process. It can be thought of as an enlargement of our knowledge by the application of something that we know already to a new situation. If we wish to explain something we know to a person who does not know, we try to find an analogy, a corresponding route in a separate field of meaning, that is known both to us and to the other person. Second, it should be realized that, although there is new knowledge, the form that this knowledge takes is not very different (in size, scale, general shape, etc.) from that which was known already. This is the nature of analogy; it is also the nature of generalization. There are many things we know that have the same form. Knowledge of the form and not merely the things makes it possible for us to know much more than we can "hold in our heads" at any one time.

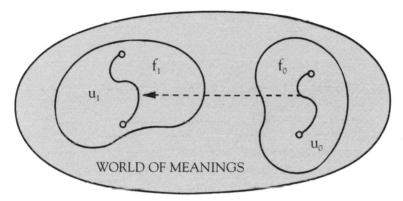

Fig. 6.2 A sketch of a world of meanings in which two fields of meaning, f_0 and f_1, are identified. The transfer of the curve of understanding, u_0, from the known field, f_0, to the new field, f_1, generates, by analogy, new knowledge, u_1.

Analogies occur in many modes among which are included models such as a scale model (a ship or a building), a representation that purports to be an identity (a model home in a real-estate development), or a map which is developed on the basis of a high level of abstraction. A photograph can be thought of as an analogue of that which it pictures. A table of organization can be thought of as an analogue of an administration. Notice that the central aspect of an analogy is that it is relational. It is not that the two lines of understanding u_1 and u_0 are, in themselves, analogies; it is rather that the relationship between them is analogical. We say that u_0 is analogous to or forms an analogy with u_1.

The creation of an analogy in the way that has been described leaves the shape or form of the world of meanings undistorted. If the map was flat to begin with, it remains flat after the analogical relationship has been established. It remains flat because we are applying an understanding already held to a field of meanings in which we lack an understanding. Therefore it is possible for the analogy to establish a new understanding that is in accord with the old. There is no tension in this situation. There is a "fit" because the new understanding, u_1, was previously unestablished; the meanings were flexible or fluid and able to conform without strain to the understanding u_0. Thus u_0 serves as a kind of mold for the creation of u_1 out of the fluid or viscous meanings that comprise f_1.

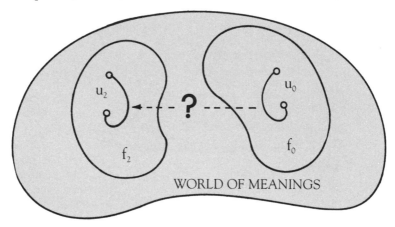

Fig. 6.3 A world of meanings shown as containing two fields of meaning each of which contains an established understanding.

Occasionally someone insists on making an analogical relationship between two understandings that are already formed, which we will call u_0 and u_2. This situation is depicted in Fig. 6.3. As the figure attempts to show, there is no analogical relationship here. What is the result of an insistence that these two understandings u_0 and u_2 are analogous? We leave aside, for the moment, the warrant for such an insistence and concentrate our attention on the result of this insistence. The insistence sets up a strain in our world of meanings. How can u_0 and u_2 be made analogous? We might try to stretch the map, to pull it as if it were a rubber sheet. In the example shown, is it possible to imagine

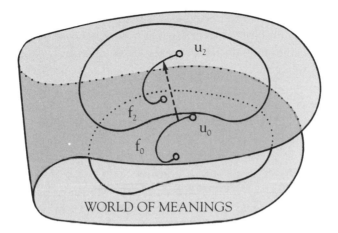

WORLD OF MEANINGS

Fig. 6.4 A fold in a map of a world of meanings (see Fig. 6.3) that
makes an analogical relationship between the two understandings u_0 and u_2 possible. This permanent folding is the result of
a metaphor that has become assimilated and has the effect of
reordering the relationships between other understandings not
shown in the illustration.

how the sheet might be pulled out of shape in order to make the
two understandings correspond? It is not apparent that any reasonably limited distortion of the flat map will achieve this. But
we must go further. The map of the world of meanings must be
folded over on itself, that is, taken out of the flat plane in which
it has been held and bent over upon itself so that the field f_2 lies
"above" the field f_0. (See Fig. 6.4) The metaphoric process is responsible for these distortions. With the fields distorted in the
way we have shown, it becomes possible to see an analogical relationship between u_0 and u_2. But look at what had to be done to
achieve this. We have forced an analogy where none existed,
with the result that our world of meanings has been bent out of
shape. We have created a metaphor. The finding of analogies
may arrange or rearrange the concepts that populate our fields of
meanings, but the metaphoric process reforms fields of meanings
themselves. There is a sense in which analogies are found—they
either exist or do not exist. Metaphors, by contrast, are created.
When worlds of meaning are willfully distorted, what is the case

was not the case earlier and what was the case no longer is. The metaphorical relationship arises when we *insist* that the relationship between "already understoods" is analogical. The effect of this insistence is to warp, distort, fold, spindle, and perhaps mutilate our world of meanings. What an outrage!

What possible grounds can we have for this violence? We do it because we know that the relationship is true, because we know that the process will work, or at least we claim such knowledge. What might be the motive or ground for such a claim? It is here that the idea of disclosure comes up again; it is here that the words "Eureka, I have it!" are spoken. At this point an "ontological flash" occurs. Some might wish to say inspiration. Two examples will describe what we mean: The first is intended to transmit an intuitive sense of the experience of the ontological flash; the second is intended to be more explanatory.

Some years ago we were rummaging around in the dark attic of a house on a stormy night. We had been told that we would find a certain chair in the attic, and we had been groping along for some time. Our hands had encountered a variety of objects which we were more or less able to identify: an old bridge lamp, a cedar chest, some old clothes on a hanger. Suddenly, there was a flash of lightning, and for a split second the entire attic was full of light. Then it was dark again. From that instant on we knew where all of the objects in the attic were. We were able to go, with confidence, right to the spot where the chair had been placed.

For the second example, imagine that we have, for our entire lives, lived and moved in the world with the aid of the sight from only one eye. We would see the world as having no depth. That is, the naïve understanding of our immediate experience of the world would be an understanding of the world as a two-dimensional picture. Over the years, however, we observe that some objects overlap others and our experience is that those "in front" appear to move faster as we move than do those objects "in back." As a result of considerable reflection on these many experiences we begin to understand the ideas of perspective and parallax, and we develop a mediated understanding of what we see as having the dimension of depth.

Now imagine that, just for a brief moment, we see through two eyes. In that moment we experience the full sense of the perception of depth that can come from binocular vision, the miracle of the stereopticon. We have the equivalent of an ontological flash. We believe in this instant that we see "face-to-face." This vision distorts our world of meanings; it takes a naïve understanding of a new experience and insists that it conform to our mediated understanding of another experience. In so doing it warps our map of the world of meanings. We have come to know by means of metaphor.

These examples show how an ontological flash can be the basis for an insistence on making a metaphor. Now we examine, from a slightly different perspective, motives for making a metaphor.

Not in every case of making a metaphor does one have such a dramatic experience as an ontological flash. More often, we do not have a limit experience of that kind. Our situation is more likely one of having a hunch, a tentative idea that seems promising. Somehow, perhaps for a variety of reasons, it seems to us that one understanding ought to be analogous to another understanding. What we might do in this case is to fly a trial balloon. We might make a metaphor and see whether it grabs anyone. What have we to lose by messing around in the world of meanings, bending a little here, stretching a little there, or even ripping the whole thing to shreds? Perhaps our metaphor will seize a few other minds. Perhaps if we are extraordinarily lucky it will even resonate with an entire generation. In the business of making a metaphor, there is also a quality of trying it out to see if it works.

The map of the world of meanings serves as a means of explicating the genesis and operation of analogies and metaphors; the ways in which topological aspects of this two-dimensional world are affected by the function of metaphor clarify as well what happens to metaphors after they have been created. Some metaphors are so successful that they make an irreversible alteration in our world of meanings in the sense of changing its shape in such a way as to make possible a permanent analogical relationship between the two initial understandings. This situation is illustrated in Fig. 6.4. Here the world of meanings has been profoundly altered by the success of the metaphor which has itself become an analogy now that the folding of the map has reduced the tension between u_0 and u_2. Our world of meanings has been given a permanent press.

There are two other possible outcomes for a metaphor. Some metaphors maintain the strain in the world of meanings that results from not being able to establish a satisfactory or entirely descriptive analogical relationship between u_0 and u_2. The result is that the problematic (and potentially fruitful) relationship is maintained with the ongoing possibility of new meanings. The metaphor God is love, if it is properly understood, continues to live as a metaphor, whereas the well-known "all the world's a stage" that we quoted earlier from Shakespeare has largely completed a permanent wrinkle in the world of meanings with the result that much of its tension has been lost, and we make the analogy of world and stage with ease.

The second possibility for a metaphor is death. In the case of a dead metaphor the world of meanings has lost tension and possibly analogy as well. When we say, with MacCormac, that "time flies" we make an assertion that previously demanded an analogical relationship between two fields of meanings: the passage of time, and the flight of birds. The effect of the death of the metaphor is to "pin" the world of meanings at this point as if one had stitched the two parts of the map together. This attachment of one part of the surface to another in a direct stitching changes the topological character of the world of meanings so that one can move from birds to flight to time without ever consciously encountering an analogical relationship. One has, in effect, moved smoothly from one surface to another, and the understanding of "flies" is as intimately related to "time" as it is to "birds." This process is basic to human understanding and, as we shall see in chapter eight, has ontological import as well. The process is called lexicalization when only the linguistic aspects are being considered.

Just as the making of a metaphor is not limited to the linguistic, neither is the unstitching of a dead metaphor. Sallie McFague's *Metaphorical Theology: Models of God in Religious Language* (1982) is a sensitive effort to undo the patriarchalism which has resulted from the death (literalization) of the classical religious metaphor,

God the father.[21] The audacity of relating the sacred and the human in this (at one time) live metaphor can still be sensed in the scriptural portrayal of Jesus suggesting that the disciples pray, "Our father in heaven. . . ." But whereas the scriptures presented Jesus as being free from all trappings of power and authority for their own sake ("Call no man father"), in the religious tradition patriarchy became the unreflective norm for human behavior. McFague emphasized the "two-way traffic in ideas" by which she meant that, just as God the father became normative through Biblically-denominated roles (such as those of judge, king, and husband), males but not females found an identity and a goal which was beyond the possibility of fulfillment. But the task of undoing this metaphor which has dominated the Judaic and Christian traditions so completely is formidable. The surest way to unstitch a metaphor is to create new tension with a new metaphor. To unstitch the equation of God and father and to make room for other understandings would require the introduction of stronger metaphors, and in this case any replacement would have to be extraordinarily powerful. It remains to be seen whether McFague's somewhat "tame" model of God as friend is strong enough to re-position that of God the father, which like "time flies," has lost the tension of conflicting fields of meanings and has changed the character of our world. Nevertheless, McFague's documentation of the need to overcome the permanent distortion in the world of religious meanings by the dead metaphor God the father is a clear example of one phase of the metaphoric process.

Metaphors, we have claimed, do not have to be constructed with words. They abound in the graphic arts, in political cartoons, in advertising images, and in more serious artistic efforts such as the paintings of René Magritte or the drawings of M. C. Escher. We choose one of the latter for our example of a visual metaphor. Fig. 6.5 is a reproduction of a woodcut done by Escher in 1937. We offer a verbal description of the woodcut and we find, among other things, that a visual metaphor is weakened by a translation just as a verbal one is.

In the woodcut we see a table with personal articles (cards, pipe, matches, tobacco jar) and a group of books in the middle of which is a narrow city street such as one might find in Paris or

Fig. 6.5 "Still Life and Street" by M. C. Escher.

Rome. The field of meanings associated with the street (commerce, conversation, washing, children at play) is conjoined with the field of meanings associated with an accidental grouping of books on a study table (reading for relaxation, amusement, the comfort of a pipe) to create the world of imagination to be found in vicarious travel of the armchair peripatetic. The effect of the metaphor is, of course, to open up the worlds of reading.

• •

This explication of the metaphoric process, together with the ways in which the process alters both worlds and fields of meanings, will be the key to understanding the most significant similarities between science and religion.

It is easier to understand how knowledge increases by means of analogy than it is to understand how new knowledge arises metaphorically. It is of particular importance to see that it is the theoretical structure of the meanings involved in metaphor that makes new knowledge possible. The distortion of the fields of meanings by means of the metaphoric process is a structural change which demands that other meanings and understandings have to be changed in the wake of the metaphor. This is what is so different about the metaphoric process. Analogy, on the other hand, is an extension of meaning (as distinct from the creation of new meaning). The increased knowledge from analogy is primarily in terms of the original understandings.

The epistemological role of metaphor rarely surfaces in the theories of metaphor examined earlier, however. Only in Aristotle and in Ricoeur did we find explicit reference to the excellence of metaphor as compared with analogy. Hesse, Barbour, and MacCormac, pioneers in the application of metaphor to science, found no essential difference between metaphor and analogy.

The metaphoric act distorts a world of meanings in such a way as to make possible an analogical relationship between one known and another known, an analogical relationship that was not possible before the metaphoric distortion took place. In the absence of metaphor, an analogy is limited to being between a known and an unknown because one of the two must be adjustable (i.e., the unknown is not established in its field of meanings). An analogical relationship may be discovered to exist between two knowns. The discovery of an analogy between two knowns is not an epistemological act that changes either knowledge or the world of meanings. In such a case, analogy is an accidental correspondence, something like finding out that a half dollar happens exactly to cover a poker chip. The situation of interest is the one where there is no present analogical relationship, and where it is fruitful to create a metaphor, a distortion of the world of meanings, so that there will be an uncalled-for analogy between the two knowns. It is not the understanding of the knowns that changes. A change has occurred because a newly structured world of meanings causes us to see the world "through new spectacles."

In the discussion of a possible motive for doing metaphoric violence to our worlds of meanings, we have introduced the term "ontological flash." The term has the capacity to give a sense of the tension before and after new meaning is created. However, it is not yet clear from either the descriptions (as related to disclosure, the Eureka experience, inspiration) or the examples (the flash of lightning in a dark attic, the experience of a one-eyed person momentarily experiencing binocular vision) just how the flash is, in a theoretical sense, ontological.

But before we go on to take up the ontological issues latent in our theory of metaphor, we present in the next chapter representative examples of metaphor in religion and in science. Our theory of metaphor is then used as a basis for analyzing each of these examples.

CHAPTER SEVEN

Two Metaphors

Cᴀɴ ᴛʜɪѕ ᴛʜᴇᴏʀʏ of metaphor illuminate our experiences and understandings of the emergence of new meaning? Two metaphors—the concept of life-after-death in religion and the special theory of relativity in science—are presented and then examined in the light of the theory of metaphor designed in the previous chapter.

A RELIGIOUS METAPHOR

One of the most widely read atheistic philosophers of the late 1960's and early 1970's, Ernst Bloch, described his political plans for the future in his book, *Man on His Own* (1971):

> The course of liberation . . . is thus not aimed at facilitating somnolence or generalizing the pleasurable, comfortable leisure of the contemporary upper classes. We do not propose to end up with the world of Dickens, or to warm ourselves at the fireplaces of Victorian England, at best. The goal . . . is this: to give to every human not just a job but his own distress, boredom, wretchedness, misery, and darkness, his own buried, summoning light; to give to everyone's life a Dostoevskyan touch, so that each will be clear about himself and his moral party-affiliation once the walls of the body tumble—[the walls] of the world body that shielded us from the demons—in other words, once the ramparts of the realm of earthly institutions are razed.[1]

Although he called himself an atheist, Bloch's work had unmistakable apocalyptic mainsprings, and his own summary statement—"S is not yet P"—was cited by many thinkers as pertaining to the central religious insight of our time. His radical emphasis, as he used the Judaic and Christian doctrines of eschatology, was on the bounding of the present by a future—by which he meant that a future not only enters into the present, moment by moment, but discloses the present to be at once unfinished and in need of completion.

One of the most common religious metaphors, one which informs the theological theories of eschatology, is life-after-death. Eschatology (knowledge of last things) is best understood, not in the sense of an everyday knowledge of facts about the future (for example, when and where I will die; when, where, and how the present world will end), but in the sense of projecting a future which is intrinsic to human freedom and the operations of consciousness. This projective view is grounded for the religious person in an understanding of the meaning of conversion, which may be described as the awareness that the self possesses an openness toward the future "not merely as fact and achievement, but as gift."[2]

There exists today among theologians from many traditions a consensus that eschatology need not include a literal belief in life after death, either individually or anthropologically. Indeed, when one studies even classical theological interpretations in the Christian tradition, one finds that there is not an easy relationship among the last things whatever they are taken to be. Schleiermacher, a nineteenth-century theologian, for example, spoke of four last things: the return of Christ, general resurrection, judgment, and eternal blessedness (eternal damnation he handled in an appendix).[3] He strongly cautioned against understanding the "last things" separate from the domain of the inner life. By the "last things" we mean the theoretical relationships among the different aspects of our limit-thoughts about the future as they impinge upon the present.

The notion of life-after-death appears often in the beliefs, symbols, and images of several major traditions. The meaning of life-after-death tends to be lost, however, when the image is translated into concept. With the assistance of an epistemological theory of metaphor and the concept of naïveté, as developed in chapters four through six, an appropriate theological understanding of life-after-death, a phenomenon that pushes at the boundaries of thought, becomes possible.

Each major religion has a different image for the idea of life-after-death. Perhaps the oldest image of the afterlife is the kingdom of Osiris of the Egyptians.[4] How did one get to the kingdom of Osiris? According to one view, the soul set out sturdily with staff in hand to begin its long march up the valley which led to the long Oasis road. The Oasis was the frontier of the unknown. Beyond it, lay the end of the world, the mountains where the sun leaves the visible world to enter the Duat, the underworld of stars. There the fortunate soul could sit at ease under the shade trees, watching his slaves plough the black earth with oxen or reap the enormous ears of maize from grain twelve feet tall, while he conversed with his friends or played a leisurely game of checkers with his smiling wife.

A different image informs the two-thousand-year-old Hindu doctrine of rebirth. A substantial and imperishable soul goes, through death, from one existence to another, its direction and status absolutely determined from existence to existence by the inescapable and inflexible law of karma. By this law, rebirth takes place when the soul-substance passes over from one existence to another—hence, the doctrine of reincarnation or the transmigration of souls. Buddha revised the doctrine of reincarnation, however, teaching that a karma-laden character structure passes over to the next life when someone dies. What does this mean? Karma has been compared to a design made by a seal pressed upon wax. When the soul passes from the former life to the afterlife, only the abstract design which the wax obtained from the seal passes over. With respect to rebirth, Buddha taught that nothing substantial was retained and that the characteristics possessed by an individual were impressed on a new existence in another womb.[5]

In Christianity the idea of life-after-death is complex and no longer necessarily linked to a temporal sequence. The image of life-after-death is contextualized in the Christian scriptures by belief in the Kingdom of God. In the sayings ascribed to Jesus there was the radical expectation, not so much that the Kingdom would occur in time to come after the present, but that the Kingdom was to be found within humans themselves. In the early Christian community there was a strong belief in the Second Coming. Jesus as the representation of God on earth would soon return as a judge of all humans. Later, however, the imminence of the Second Coming was understood to be an unverified literalization of the meaning of the Kingdom of God.

All these images express a struggle to understand the central idea of life-after-death. Paul, for example, referring to himself as the last of the apostles, said that he was "born when no one expected it."[6] The meaning here seems to be that he became alive when he became an apostle, which suggests that his existence previous to this conversion was not life but death. In another passage he spoke of all persons as "dying in Adam and being brought to life in Christ" as though Adam had not in fact been the biblical ancestor through whom life had been given.[7] Again, speaking about the manner of resurrection, Paul asserted that "we are not all going to die, but we shall all be changed." Or again, "the trumpet shall sound, and the dead will be raised."[8]

Now in what sense are these expressions of life-after-death metaphorical? In relation to a world of meanings, the notion of life-after-death introduces a fundamental twist or torque in the day-to-day ordinary perception of reality. As a result of an ontological flash or insight into the problem of the equivalence of life and death, we grapple with the fact of our own death complicated by the sense in which we view death from within life. The central metaphor, life-after-death, boggles the mind with its opacity. The inability to reduce one to the other or to conceive of what either might be, taken without the other, constitutes a more or less sustained tension in one's world of everyday meanings.

At the same time, in relation to the fields of meanings, the metaphor jars the imagination. No ordinary biological or chemical denotation will elicit the totality of meanings implied in the metaphor. Fig. 7.1 illustrates the clash of meanings which occurs when all of the ideas associated with the field of death are imposed upon all of the ideas associated with the field of life. The religious expression, life-after-death, introduces a sustained tension among other fields of meanings. That is, the religious mean-

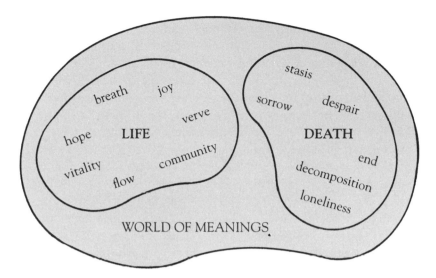

Fig. 7.1 A world of meanings containing one field of meanings related to the concept of life and another field of meanings related to the concept of death.

ing keeps its relationship to the ordinary meanings but introduces a new meaning which clashes with everyday meanings of the terms. Religious persons who have faced the fact of their own death and who have also wrestled with the conflict between the biological meaning of human death and the religious expression life-after-death are on the threshold of a new understanding of life, because death is now involved in the meaning of life, or as one Christian burial service puts it, "In the midst of life we are in death." This new understanding also suggests a new way of being, because the new congruence seen between my death and my life assimilates me in the very knowing of the congruence. As Ricoeur said, "We feel *like* what we see *like*." In other words, persons who understand the tensive character of the religious expression, life-after-death, place themselves differently in life after the limit-experience than they did before.

The analysis of metaphor in theological terms provides a conceptual space for the tension of the metaphor to be felt and assimilated throughout one's world of meanings. This tension can be confronted in at least three ways: (1) One can use the tension to contradict one's ordinary world of meanings and to conclude in paradox; (2) One can succumb to the tension, allowing it to bring about a horizon-shift so sudden and radical that self-continuity is sacrificed; (3) One can mediate the new meaning, allowing it to transform the new incompatibility within the self's steady horizon-growth. However the tension is assimilated, a person's life is changed whenever a metaphor forces a change in that person's world of meanings. If we change the world of meanings, we change the theory (in Hanson's sense). That is, when we look at something after the metaphoric process has taken place, our observation is different from what it was before. Kuhn might say that we have been subjected to a paradigm-shift.

The tension between two or more fields of meanings is lost either when one of the terms is removed or when the distinction is not preserved and one term is subsumed into the other. We have graphic examples of the ways in which life-after-death has become literalized. From the grand pyramids which the pharoahs built to prepare themselves for their voyage to the after-life, tombs complete with food, money, and favorite possessions, to the medieval obsession with relics and indulgences, to our own concern for satin-lined, water-tight caskets, for embalmed corpses with comfortable shoes, we witness the absence of tension between the referents of life and death. Not so many years ago a group of concerned citizens in Cleveland, Ohio, allowed their cemetery to take on the aspects of a city, with mausoleums built to resemble miniature buildings. Most of us have heard casual comments to the effect that "this cemetery would be perfect, except that the railroad tracks are too close by," the implication being that the last resting place should not be noisy!

Only by refusing to conflate the terms of a metaphor—refusing to substitute "afterlife" for "life-after-death"—can one sustain its tensive meaning. Conflation of terms and loss of the tension occurs both within and outside religious traditions. Someone looking in on another's attempts to grapple with the tension of metaphor, wherein new meanings occur because of new relationships among things that were not formerly associated, may perceive instability—something like being half-way up a lightly greased pole.

It is a curious and significant feature of religious metaphors that no matter how deeply they fall into myth or literalization, they remain remarkably retrievable in all their sinewy tension and stubborn opaqueness so long as they are understood as metaphor. The durability of religious metaphors does not in itself preclude naïveté, however, with respect to understanding of those metaphors. Merely to accept the idea of life-after-death without any further questions results in a first naïveté for the individual and in a literalization of the belief. Failure to recognize the theoretical structure as theoretical and to question it in terms of one's own horizon of understanding results in a second naïveté. Merely to accept the notion of karma or of the Kingdom of God without asking why one understands and believes in terms of this particular theoretical explanation and with this root-metaphor results in second naïveté and ossification of the beliefs.

The notion of first naïveté is equally applicable in a positive sense to both religious and scientific metaphors. For if knowledge-in-process is the condition for the possibility of cognitive self-transcendence, the individual must develop the art of moving away from immediate awarenesses. For this reason, a too facile indictment of first naïveté is to be avoided. It can be misleading to speak of first naïveté in terms of mythic understanding as Mac-Cormack did, for example, when he said that myth results from the "false attribution of reality to a diaphoric metaphor."[9] Here, the sense in which the attribution is "false," or why falsity is even an issue at this point, is not clear. Moreover, if metaphor itself affects the way we see things, it does so before the issue of truth or falsity arises.

The relationship between the myth-making process and first naïveté can be appropriately understood by means of Lonergan's distinction between thing and body. In the myth-making process, theoretical structure is on its way to being understood as body. By theoretical structure we mean an abstract description involving systematic relations among all of the terms in the description. In the foregoing example of religious metaphor, the terms which are related are the biological meaning of death, a phenomenological analysis of death in the context of consciousness made explicit, and a theological understanding of the overarching central religious meanings of particular traditions. A person's understanding of a theoretical structure falls into first naïveté when the recognition of the abstract nature of the theoretical structure is forgotten or when the mediative role of the theoretical structure is lost.

Science and religion as fields of meanings are also equally susceptible to the engendering of a second naïveté. The richness of the network of meanings available can obscure the need to ask questions about questions and the need to recognize the matter-of-fact limitations of any particular inquiry in terms of the questions we can ask and can't answer.

In the past, the dichotomization of science and religion contributed to the fostering of second naïveté in both science and religion. Traditional science has restricted its progress to questions of how something happened to the exclusion of questions of why something happened. Traditional religion, on the other hand, because it has been concerned primarily with teleological significance, emphasized ultimate questions of why something happened. As a result, certain kinds of questions—namely, questions that can be asked but not answered—have been systematically eliminated from both disciplines. In science the general tendency has been to leave why questions unarticulated and, in the successful answering of all relevant how questions, to forget just how narrow the selected range of inquiry is. In religion the general tendency has been to neglect attention to how questions and often to rush in with ossified answers to why questions. "Mystery," for example, has too often been used as an untimely and inappropriate response to why questions, thereby truncating the act of inquiry.

When why questions are habitually answered in a horizon of second naïveté (as they appear to be, for example, in representative seventeenth-century religion), it is understandable that science would attempt to protect its methods for overcoming first naïveté by choosing to exclude why questions altogether. And when how questions are habitually answered in a horizon of second naïveté (as they appear to be in representative seventeenth-century science), it is understandable that religion would attempt to protect its methods for overcoming second naïveté by minimizing how questions to the point of virtually excluding them. The irony is that both disciplines incur an even more serious second naïveté of their own.

In order to allow authentic why questions to emerge in religion, religion and theology need to be distinguished. By religion we mean expression (through cultural institutions, beliefs, and rituals) of basic confidence in life and in life-context, together with a desire for liberation and authenticity.[10] By theology we mean a reflective understanding of religion, which compares, grounds, and questions the appropriateness of the images and expressions of religious belief and understanding. This differentiation between religion and theology minimally provides three alternatives for responding theologically to a why question which pertains to religious meaning: (1) We may reflect on the images of the religious tradition which is most accessible to us, comparing them with those of other traditions (probably an instance of first naïveté); (2) We may reflect on the theoretical understanding with which we are familiar, distinguishing it from other theoretical understandings (probably an instance of second naïveté); (3) We may question the theoretical understanding, reflecting on the status of the question among other questions which we ask and on the senses in which it may and may not be responded to. This is likely to engender an instance of cognitive self-transcendence or knowledge-in-process.

The effort to distinguish one theological (or theoretical) understanding from another does not result in an automatic self-transcendence. Knowledge-in-process does require that we move away from our immediate understandings, and we most easily do this by means of comparison, but comparison may also fall into naïveté. That is, failing to achieve a full understanding of the thing being investigated, the individual all too easily falls into a gnosticism (the religious equivalent of begging the question) or an uncritical pluralism, both of which inhibit further understanding and further horizon-growth.

The preservation of religious metaphor somewhat insures against second naïveté. As far as is known, wherever there is human history, there are religious questions. The problem for every age is to understand them in such a way that they are not literalized nor trivialized. It is important, for example, to retrieve the tension that traditional religious metaphors (such as life-after-death) can provide within our worlds and fields of ordinary meanings. As metaphors, these religious meanings have the potential of positioning us in such a way that we have to ask questions about questions. When religious metaphors transform one's horizon, they provide the intellectual energy necessary to question the fields of ordinary meanings in which we live out our ordinary existence. And when religious metaphors inform our horizon, they eventually force us to reach out beyond the world of cognitive meanings toward moral and religious self-transcendence.

Metaphors, recognized for what they are (but whose tensions are not resolved), demand careful preliminary analyses of our own horizon and that of the contemporary scene. Since the 1950's that possibility in the field of religion has changed considerably for the better. Information about other religions has become much more accessible. It would be a lost opportunity, however, if we were to understand data about other religions only as so much more new information with which we are intrigued or amused. Wilfred Cantwell Smith, a careful and well-known pioneer in the field of the history of religions, put the point well. The study of comparative religions today is, inescapably, humans studying themselves, accordingly to Smith. Religious diversity has come to be so much a part of contemporary life that both believers and non-believers are affected by it. Being a Christian, for example, entails the recognition that others like oneself are devout and intelligent but are Buddhists, Hindus, and Muslims. Non-religious persons as well are caught up in the phenomenon of unreconciled faiths.[11] This troubling diversity is one of the most moving and dangerous aspects of contemporary life.

If it could be presumed that all of these individuals are engaging the tension of recognized metaphors of their own traditions, we could have a greater confidence in the human efforts to live authentically in the midst of limit-experiences and limit-questions.

• •

In referring to the religious metaphor life-after-death we have used a number of religious statements or expressions of the kind listed below:

life-after-death
second birth
dying in Adam
living in Christ
death in the midst of life

Any of these expressions could, by itself, be understood as a metaphor in the conventional sense of the term. However, by focusing not on any one expression but rather on the common referent of all such expressions, we have managed to reach through the specific expressions of metaphor to the metaphoric thought itself. This situation can be expressed in another way: If we once again make use of Frege's distinction between sense and reference, we can consider all of the religious expressions of the kind listed above to have the same referent but to allude to it with different senses. Despite the presence of these many senses, these several linguistic metaphors refer to one cognitive metaphor, one distortion in our world of meanings, a distortion that can be expressed in a number of different ways.

Perhaps it is appropriate now for us to re-examine the choice of the term "distortion." The term carries with it an implicit sense of error which is not appropriate for our purposes. It might be better to say that our world of meanings is changed in shape or re-formed. In some cases the re-formation may be a topological simplification; in others it may mean an increase in complexity. In no case do we mean to imply that the new structure is, in and of itself, necessarily better or worse or more or less "true." New paradigms may be better than old but not merely because they are new.

The reference to second naïveté is especially useful as applied to the workings of science. This literalization of metaphoric understandings will be treated in more detail in a subsequent examination of the idea of the ontological in science. For the moment we will take advantage of the fact that we have an idea of meta-aphor that has been freed from its ordinary restriction to certain groups of words and examine a metaphor in science, a metaphor that will be seen not to be made up of words at all.

A SCIENTIFIC METAPHOR

To complete the application of our epistemological theory of metaphor to religion and science, it will be helpful to reiterate what we mean by analogy and metaphor in a formal way. Apply-ing these statements to the analysis of a root-metaphor in natural philosophy, we show how the creation of a metaphor distorts our world of meanings so that our understanding of nature is radically changed.

An analogy is created when we posit a conformal relationship between something that we know and something that we do not know. To posit an analogy, then, is to order what is unknown in one epistemic field in terms of what is known in another. The analogical act carried out in this way creates no tension in our epistemic world (our world of meanings) because the unknown is free to be ordered, precisely because it is unknown. Thus, to say, for example, that a puppy's fur is as soft as velvet is to presume that the softness of velvet in the epistemic field of the properties of fabrics is known and that the softness of puppy fur in the epis-temic field of the properties of animal skins is unknown. The knowledge of the softness of puppy fur is created by the analogy. If a knowledge of the softness of puppy fur does exist before the analogy is made, the analogy may be seen as satisfactory but fruitless. No new knowledge is created. On the other hand, to say that the skin of an armadillo is as soft as velvet is to create the following possibilities: (1) The character of armadillo skin is initially unknown and is now known incorrectly or, (2) the char-acter of velvet is initially unknown and is now known incor-rectly, or (3) the character of both velvet and armadillo skin is initially known and the analogy is denied.

In each of these possibilities, the analogy can be seen to be a "bad" analogy either because it creates misunderstanding or, as in the third possibility, because no analogy exists. It is precisely here that metaphor comes in.

The making of a metaphor creates a more or less permanent distortion in our field of meanings. The fundamental epistemological effect of the metaphoric process becomes clear when we realize that to think about something after the field of meanings in which it resides has been distorted means to understand that something in a necessarily different way. The metaphoric process is the primary sculptor of our thinking territory. Lakoff and Johnson claim, for example, that "Most of our fundamental concepts are organized in terms of one or more spatialization metaphors."[12] Although their examples are verbal despite the references to space, it is clear that the verbal processing they illustrate runs parallel to a more general level of thought processing. In Fig. 7.2 the fields of meanings have been distorted so that what was not analogical prior to the metaphoric insistence has become analogical after the metaphoric process has taken place.

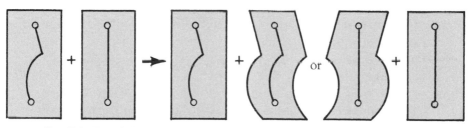

Fig. 7.2 Two fields of meanings each containing a concept not analogous to the other until after the metaphoric process distorts the fields of meanings. The figure suggests that either or both of the fields could suffer distortion, an ambiguity which contributes to the sustaining of the tension.

We say that metaphor results when one insists on an analogical relationship between concepts in separate epistemic fields in spite of the fact that both concepts are previously understood (known). It is this insistence that creates the tension in the epistemic world. What is to be made of an insistence on the fact that an armadillo's skin is as soft as velvet? Our conclusion is apt to be that the statement has been by a person who is cognitively incompetent or, at the very least, has a perspective or operates out of a paradigm that is radically different from ours. We can adopt that meaning only by distorting our own epistemic world. Herein lies both the power and the threat of metaphor. As with all strong medicines, one should have good and strong motivations for using it.

In chapter six we spoke of the conviction that can arise in the face of what we called an "ontological flash" and suggested that such events might justify metaphorical insistence. Here we limit ourselves to the analysis of a particular metaphor in physics, to a justification of our claim that it is a metaphor, and to an examination of the effect of the metaphorical act on our understanding of the world. The justification for the metaphorical insistence will be left to chapter eight.

An example of a root-metaphor in science is Einstein's Special Theory of Relativity as it was formulated in his first paper on the subject in 1905. To show that the relativity theory is a metaphor we need to show (1) that it involves concepts in two different epistemic fields, (2) that each of these concepts is understood within its own field; and (3) that the relativity theory is the result of insisting on an analogical relationship between the two concepts.

For the last property we can turn to Gerald Holton's remarks about the way Einstein typically began a scientific article: "The significant starting point is a formalistic difference between theoretical representations in two fields of physics which, to most physicists, were so widely separated that no such comparison would have invited itself . . . "[13] or, in Einstein's own words, the relativity theory grew out of " . . . an amazingly simple summary and generalization of hypotheses which previously have been independent of one another. . . ."[14] It remains, then, for us to state the situation in a form that will permit the application of the three criteria listed above.

Galilean Relativity In Newtonian Mechanics

Since the seventeenth century it has been understood that the laws of motion in the field of mechanics are independent of any constant motion of the frame of reference in which the laws are to be used. Such frames of reference, called inertial frames, may move with constant speed in any constant direction. Put in another way, this principle amounts to the assertion that in an inertial frame of reference, there is no experiment that can be performed which will serve as a means of detecting the possible motion of that reference frame.

If we are in a train on a track next to another train and we glance up to see through a window the other train moving, we are at a loss to tell whether it is our train that is in motion or the other. Furthermore, as the principle of Galilean relativity states, there is no mechanical experiment that will serve to tell us whether our train is in motion, whether the other train is in motion, or whether both trains are in motion (with respect to the tracks). All that we are able to show is that our train is in motion with respect to the other, or that it is in motion relative to the other, or that the other is in motion relative to ours. All of these statements are equivalent. If the window shade is now drawn down, we have no basis for making any statement about the possibility of uniform motion. We simply cannot know whether or not we are moving.

The paragraph above corresponds to our understanding of the concept of motion in the field of mechanics. The understood concept we can label u_0 and the epistemic field in which it occurs, namely the field of Newtonian mechanics, we can label f_0. We can say that we know the meaning of Galilean relativity u_0 in this field.

An Understanding Of This Situation In Maxwellian Electromagnetism

We now turn to a different field of meanings, the epistemic field of electromagnetism which we shall label f_2. We will now consider an experimental situation that can be understood in terms of this field, namely, the interaction of a line of charge with a single charge that is placed at rest with respect to the line of charge at a distance R from it. By means of the laws of electromagnetism we can calculate the force that will be exerted on the single charge due (as we say) to the electric field generated by the stationary line of charge. An observer would be able to measure this force by observing, in principle, the amount by which the charged particle is accelerated as a result of the interaction of the charge and the electric field. We might set up this situation by arranging for the line of charge to lie parallel to the roadbed in the train of our former example. The charge or particle would be suspended some horizontal distance R from the line of charge and our intention would be to observe any horizontal acceleration that would result from the repulsion of the charge (presumed positive) by the line of charge (presumed to be made up of positive charges).

The situation, in the event that the train, the line of charge, and the single test charge are all in motion, is curiously different. Since the line of charge is in motion, it corresponds to an electric current as if the charge were flowing through a wire strung along the direction of motion of the train. In this case we know, from our understanding of the epistemic field f_2, that a magnetic field will be generated, in addition to the electric field already present. The test charge is now seen to be moving through the magnetic field of the current with the result that there is a new magnetic force present in addition to the purely electrical one that existed in the first instance. An application of the laws of electromagnetism (our understanding of f_2) results in a determination that this new magnetic force is in the opposite direction to the electric force found earlier, that is, the magnetic force tends to counteract the purely electrical force. The net effect of adding these two forces is a reduction in the net force on the test charge, a reduction that depends on the speed of the train. Indeed, should the train approach the speed of light, our f_2 understanding of this arrangement tells us that the net force on the test charge will approach zero. We have, therefore, the two prerequisites for a metaphorical act. We have a concept u_0 (Galilean relativity) that is understood in relation to its epistemic field f_0 (mechanics) and a concept u_2 (Galilean relativity) that is understood in relation to its epistemic field f_2 (electromagnetism). It remains for Einstein to create the metaphor.

The Metaphoric Act

Einstein insisted that the laws of physics were the same for all observers regardless of their state of uniform motion and hence, Galilean relativity (u_0) in the field of mechanics (f_0) was equivalent to Galilean relativity (u_2) in the field of electromagnetism (f_2). "Impossible!" many exclaimed. After all, there is a clear and expected difference in the outcome in the two situations. In the mechanical situation (f_0) we cannot tell if the train is in motion, whereas in the electromagnetic situation (f_2) the force depends on whether the train is in motion. The force even tends to disappear as the train approaches the speed of light. We are faced with a statement that seems to be saying that the armadillo's skin is as soft as velvet. Was the man insane? What grounds could he possibly have had for making such a statement? (Grounds did exist at the time of Einstein's claim, in the form of the negative results of the Michaelson-Morley experiment, but Einstein did not use them).

Einstein's insistence on an analogous relationship between u_0 and u_2 (in this case, their equivalence) constituted a metaphoric act. The resulting distortions of our epistemic field particularly in the region of f_0 that surrounds u_0 are so extraordinary that they would not be accepted within the public world of meanings were it not for a substantial number of experimental observations that are in agreement with the relativity theory.

New Understandings

Unlike an analogy, a metaphor can create new knowledge that goes beyond the particular understandings in terms of which it was stated. Indeed a root-metaphor can so distort our epistemic world that most of our understandings have to be revised. In the case of special relativity, the greatest revisions that must be made occur in relation to our understandings of mass, space, and time, concepts which affect every other quantity in the field of mechanics (f_0). Among the new understandings are the following: (1) Time dilation: Any physical system whose behavior depends on time (such as a clock) will run more slowly if it is in motion. A biological system, for example, will develop and decay more slowly if it is in motion than if it is not. Indeed, if it is moving with the speed of light (upper limit to all motion) it will not age at all. No wonder our charge did not get repelled by the electric field of the line of charge; moving at the speed of light it did not experience the passage of time at all. Time dilation has been observed in the reduced decay rate of high-energy rapidly-moving particles as well as the loss of time of an atomic clock flown at high speed in a jet plane.

(2) Mass increase: Einstein's insistence on the equivalence of u_0 and u_2 results in the mathematical deduction that the mass of a moving object must increase. That is, objects in motion with respect to an observer are more massive than they would be if they were at rest with respect to the same observer. Mass increase with speed has been observed in particle accelerators. It is a problem that must be taken into account in their design, especially in the case of accelerators of electrons.

(3) Length contraction: The length of an object in motion will be reduced, by virtue of that motion, along a line in the direction of motion. This effect has been called the Lorentz-Fitzgerald contraction in honor of two natural philosophers who first proposed that such an effect might occur.

(4) The speed of light in empty space is the same for all observers regardless of the relative state of motion of the source of light and the observer. This means, for example, that if an object were traveling towards us at one-half the speed of light and a beam of light left it to travel in our direction, the beam would speed away from the object with the speed of light and approach us with the same speed regardless of the fact that the object itself was approaching us already at half that speed.

It should be borne in mind that all of the effects mentioned, except for the last, can be easily observed only at very high speeds, close to the speed of light. The effects are understood to be true at ordinary speeds even though they are too small to be detected. We can now understand why the conclusions of ordinary Newtonian mechanics were not challenged at an earlier time.

The insistence that the laws of physics must be the same for all observers without regard for their state of uniform motion formed the basis of a required relationship between a previous understanding of a mechanical experience and a previous understanding of an electromagnetic experience. The distortion of the epistemic world that resulted from this insistence so changed our understanding that where previously time was thought to be invariant and the speed of light was thought to depend on one's state of motion, now time is understood to depend on one's state of motion and the speed of light is invariant. This inversion can be seen to correspond to the metaphoric distortion that resulted in a folding of the epistemic world as illustrated earlier. That such a folding introduces a tension or stress is amply demonstrated by the reluctance with which special relativity was accepted by the scientific community. As Holton remarked, "Poincaré, who was perhaps technically the best-prepared scientist in the world to understand Einstein's relativity theory of 1905, did not deign to refer to it once in his large published output up to his death in 1912." With respect to most other scientists of the time, Holton said, "Their writings show what an outrage was being committed on their own thematic orientation. . . ."[15] What does it take to justify the commission of such an "outrage"? What gives a natural philosopher such as Einstein the justification for the epistemological havoc that he wrought? The answer lies at the heart of what Tracy called a "limit-situation," what Ramsey termed a "disclosure," and what we have called an "ontological flash." All of these relate to an idea associated with our use of the term "horizon." In the next chapter we will consider in more detail how these ideas relate to the knowledge we acquire when we inquire about the universe in which we find ourselves.

• •

By focusing on the "nascent moment" of new meaning experienced by a specific person, Albert Einstein, we have discovered an example of scientific metaphor. Metaphoric tension may be experienced by anyone who understands the concepts of motion in the two separate fields of Galilean relativity in mechanics and electromagnetism and is capable of putting the two concepts together. Einstein's insistence upon putting two fields together in the metaphoric act that created the Special Theory of Relativity might not have been persuasive to the entire scientific community, however, were it not "for a substantial number of experimental observations" that could be understood in terms of relativity theory. Not everyone can be expected to experience the nascent moment or be convinced by it.

Our example of religious metaphor similarly focused on the "nascent moment" of new meaning experienced by a specific person, Paul of Tarsus. The metaphoric tension may be experienced by anyone who understands the concepts of life and death in their two separate fields of meanings and is capable of putting the two concepts together. The metaphoric tension of life-after-death is not sustained by everyone in every religious community, and the metaphor is also capable of being understood naïvely. For those who preserve the metaphoric tension, the metaphoric understanding of life-after-death is persuasive, however, in the light of such criteria as those which James suggested (immediate luminousness, philosophical reasonableness, moral helpfulness).

If we compare the results of the metaphoric act with other kinds of extraordinary language and meaning, a metaphor in both science and religion appears to be more like an oxymoron than like a simile, more like a paradox than an analogy. But whereas the oxymoron (e.g., "a savage gentleness") stretches the ordinary understandings of qualities and whereas the paradox ("This statement expresses a lie.") proposes a disparity between ordinarily logical propositions, the metaphor, we have said, distorts not only two or more fields of meanings which have been forced together but our ordinary worlds of meanings as well.

One significant difference between the foregoing representative religious and scientific metaphors begins to emerge in this chapter and will be treated more extensively in chapter nine: It is the cognitive status of the metaphoric meanings. Another way this issue could be raised would be to ask the question of the referent of each kind of metaphor. Does the distinction between the kinds of models employed in science and religion extend to metaphors as well? Is the referent of the metaphor of the Special Theory of Relativity of a different kind than the referent of the metaphor of life-after-death?

In the next chapter, we begin to answer the question of the referents of these two metaphors by examining the ontological aspects of scientific and religious metaphors.

CHAPTER EIGHT

Ontologies

O<small>UR EMPHASIS</small> up to now has been on the ways in which we come to know in religion and science. When the soprano sings "I know that my redeemer liveth," we have not asked, "Who is your redeemer?" We have asked, rather, "How do you come to know?" But now the time has come for us to turn to that which is known. We do so, however, with the understanding that what one knows depends on how one knows, just as what one finds depends on where one looks. One does not find potatoes on the branches and apples underground. And so now we look to that which is known and finally to that which is. And this leads us to ontology.

TOWARD AN UNDERSTANDING OF THE
ONTOLOGICAL ASPECTS OF NATURAL PHILOSOPHY

We are told that Ernst Mach, one of the major natural philosophers of the second half of the nineteenth century, "died in 1916 without abandoning his view that atoms were, at best, a convenient fiction."[1] Einstein died in 1955 without abandoning his view that quantum mechanics was not an adequate description of the submicroscopic world. Poincaré, as we have observed, could not bring himself to espouse Einsteinian relativity. Here were three of the most penetrating minds of the past hundred years, and they were in great disagreement about "the way things are." What could be the grounds for this ontological alienation? What causes one scientist to deny an existence in the face of two hundred years of supporting evidence and another to believe an existence on virtually no grounds at all? To examine these ques-

141

tions we must review once more the processes that enter into scientific investigation.

Earlier we said that direct experience does not play a central
role in the practice of a mature science. Understandings, that is,
have a basis in theory and a theoretical understanding constitutes an integral part of our world of meanings. The product of
scientific investigation is an enlargement of this world of meanings. Enlargement takes place first on the individual level and
later on the community level.

The enlargement of our world of meanings that we described
in chapter four takes place at the external horizon, the boundary
between the known-known and the penumbral known-unknown,
or between the known-unknown and the unknown-unknown.
These boundaries are depicted in Fig. 8.1. There are, however,
other regions of the known-unknown that lie within the world of
the known-known and are completely surrounded by the latter.

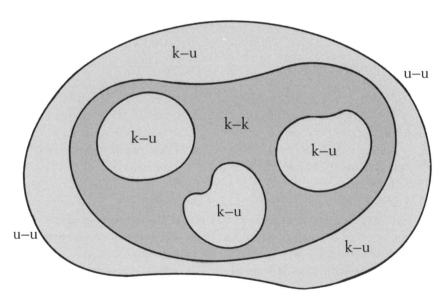

Fig. 8.1 The world of meanings showing the boundaries between the
known-known (k-k), the known-unknown (k-u), and the unknown-unknown (u-u).

In the figure these regions look like holes in our world of meanings and make the world of meanings seem more like a slice of
swiss cheese than a slice of bologna. These holes or impacted regions of the known-unknown differ from the perimeter band of
the known-unknown because the impacted regions share no
boundary with the unknown-unknown. For this reason we are
less likely to be surprised by the results of investigations that take
place in the impacted regions.

By what process of scientific investigation are these holes in
our world of meanings closed? It is here that the hypothetico-
deductive method is so effective. Earlier we rejected Bertrand
Russell's description of the scientific process as one composed of
three main stages: first, observing the significant facts; second,
arriving at a hypothesis which, if true, will account for those
facts; and third, deducing from this hypothesis consequences
which can be tested by observation.' Which facts, we asked, are
significant? We are now in a position to see that the question can
be answered in the case of investigations that are being carried
out well within the boundaries of our world of meanings. These
limited regions of the known-unknown are surrounded by the
known-known and the surroundings give an adequate basis, a
context, for choosing facts and framing hypotheses. These are
the regions in which most scientific investigation goes on. In this
interior territory the laws are well known and the primary process is deductive. The properties of new materials are studied in
the same terms as the old—new conductivities are measured;
new coefficients are determined. The theoretical trees are
shaken, and the fruits of analysis fall into the eager hands of the
harvesters.

Russell was not wrong; he merely failed to tell the whole story.
There is some truth in every honest philosophy, and these truths
will get lost if, in our eagerness to assert a novel view, we challenge, overcome, and then discard those that have come before.
The hypothetico-deductive method of scientific advance is the
one most widely used, and we should not be surprised to find that
most scientists operate a mopping up action on the level of second naïveté. They hold their truths to be self-evident.

Ontology is the science of being: It is the study of the way things are. Ontology raises questions of existence and reality. What is real for us as individuals or as a community depends, in large measure, on the way in which we encounter the world. For the scientist who is not on the front lines, who is filling in the interstices, there exists a kind of creeping ontology, an expanding realm of being that closes and mends the gaps in the world of meanings. However, it is also in these peaceful backwaters that metaphor can strike.

Consider the case of the kinetic theory of gases. Gases have been studied in a systematic way since the investigations of Robert Boyle in the latter part of the seventeenth century. The early investigations showed an inverse relationship between pressure and volume. Subsequent experiments by Jacques Charles and Joseph Gay-Lussac at the beginning of the nineteenth century demonstrated a direct relationship between volume and temperature at constant pressure. These studies, together, made it possible to write a mathematical expression that "governed" the behavior of a permanent gas:

$$PV = nRT.$$

This equation, which states that the product of the pressure and volume of a gas is proportional to the absolute temperature, is called the equation of state of the gas. Actually, it is the equation of state of an ideal gas. The "ideal" suggests that the experimenters encountered deviations from perfection which they ascribed to the properties of the different gases being investigated. These deviations, as we shall see, were significant in the development of the later atomic models for gases.

In the equation of state we find both intrinsic and extrinsic variables. An intrinsic quantity or variable is one whose magnitude is independent of the amount of material considered. Pressure and temperature are intrinsic variables. Extrinsic variables depend on the amount of material. Volume and n (which depends on the mass of the gas) are both extrinsic variables. R, a universal constant, has the same numerical value in all circumstances.

James Prescott Joule, in the middle of the nineteenth century, was interested in the relationship between heat, an extrinsic variable, and temperature, an intrinsic one. He was able to show that heat was a form of mechanical work, which meant that heat had to be understood as a form of energy. He reasoned that if a volume of gas at a particular pressure were allowed to expand into empty space it would not lose or gain energy. He showed experimentally that when such an expansion took place there was no change in the temperature even though both the pressure and the volume changed. From this he concluded that the temperature was a measure of the internal energy of the gas. However, since the energy in a gas is an extrinsic quantity (there is twice as much energy in twice as much gas) and since the temperature is an intrinsic quantity (there is no change in temperature when the amount of gas considered is twice as large), the temperature must be related to the energy of a particular sub-unit of the gas. The temperature thus became associated with the energy of an "atom" of gas whereas the heat was associated with the energy of the total amount of gas present. In a similar way, the pressure of the gas (an intrinsic variable) was understood to be related to the total force (an extrinsic variable) that the gas exerted on the walls of any container, and force is a mechanical quantity.

It was therefore possible for the theorists of the nineteenth century, scientists such as Rudolf Clausius, James Clerk Maxwell and Ludwig Boltzmann, to develop a mechanical theory of gases called the kinetic theory. In this theoretical framework gases are understood to be composed of atoms or minute particles which have, associated with each way they can move (each degree of freedom), an amount of energy that is proportional to the temperature of the gas that they comprise. From their resulting energy of motion it is possible to compute the average force that these atoms exert on any wall of their container and therefore to calculate the pressure associated with a given volume of gas at a particular temperature. From such a calculation, based entirely on the model of a gas as composed of these atoms, the kinetic theorists were able to derive (deduce) the above equation of state, an equation originally determined empirically.

Furthermore, as experimentalists examined the relationship between heat and temperature for a large number of gases, they came to realize that more heat was required to raise the temperature of some gases than was predicted by the atomic model. In these instances the theorists were able to show that this effect could be accounted for by describing the particles as more complex combinations of atoms (diatomic or polyatomic molecules) that could "partition" their allotment of energy in more ways than could the individual atoms, e.g., by rotating or vibrating so that any one degree of freedom or any one particular way of motion had less energy associated with it, with the result that a given amount of energy (heat) resulted in less motion in any one direction (temperature).

As the description progressed, as the experiments were done and explained by the developing model for a gas, the sense that this was a model gradually receded from the consciousness of the scientists and they came to "believe in" the theoretical atoms (all of them did, that is, except Mach).

From the understanding of a gas as composed of submicroscopic particles that behaved in accordance with the laws of mechanics they could deduce a large variety of situations, properties, and behaviors, all of which they observed in detail in the experimental laboratories of the late nineteenth century. Here is the working of the hypothetico-deductive process at its finest. Here were scientists immersed in a field of understanding closing in on the gaps that remained. They had entered this field by means of a metaphor that had forced an analogical relationship between atomic particles (understood within the field of mechanics) and the behavior of gases (understood within the field of thermodynamic processes) and had worked this metaphor to death. It was dead, that is, for all but a few recalcitrants like Mach, for whom the epistemic tension remained.

For the rest, however, atoms *were*. They had become ontological givens—not overnight but over the course of the years as the deductive investigations rolled on. This is creeping ontology, a kind of reality by immersion. Its validation comes from the deductive analysis which is reasonable by virtue of its form. Its verification comes by means of experimental observation, repeatable over and over again in any place and at any time. The result is ubiquitous second naïveté in the deduced effects, in the experiments, in the classrooms. This is the naïve realism that constitutes most scientific understanding. This is Bertrand Russell's science.

For most persons, that which is—the ontological dimension of existence—is comprised of the naïve understandings of immediate experience. Everything is body. For most scientists, that which is is comprised of theoretical understandings that go unquestioned—of course, there are atoms! It is no longer a question of how the world is understood; this is the way the world is. And we can from hypotheses and we can make deductions and we can observe what we expect to observe.

There remain those who continue to question. They understand the theories. They are able to make the deductions, and they agree with the experiments. However, for these scientists, these natural philosophers, the world does not quite come together as it should. So broad is their understanding that they are aware of defects that cannot be seen by those close to the fabric. They are dissatisfied with the limited quality of the truths that can be expressed. They seek understandings that are not limited to one particular field of human thought. They are unable to resist the demand for understandings that apply more broadly, that take on the character of universals.

These are the metaphor makers who bring together two or more understandings and weld them into a higher level understanding. What are the characteristics of their ontologies?

The insights that come at this highest level are not rational, that is, they cannot be derived or deduced by any systematic method. The assertions that are made by the metaphor makers cannot be validated by reasoning from premises. Verification must wait on the gradual assimilation of the new understanding on the part of the community addressed. This comes about after the fact of utterance through the questioning of the community. Those addressed listen, question, examine, experiment and finally either accept or reject. If the result is acceptance, the metaphoric distortion becomes *de rigeur* and the community accepts the new theoretical reality at the level of second naïveté. The metaphor dies.

If the understanding is rejected, then it remains individual and personal. It may perish with the originator or it may be carried on as a vague belief of a mystical nature held by members of another community, who do not perhaps have the background to question.

There remains another route to being, one that is not immediate in the way that first naïveté is immediate, nor theoretical in the way that the hypothetico-deductive mode in second naïveté is theoretical, one that does not have the iconoclastic characteristic of metaphor. We refer to the route of the pattern finder. We have neglected this way of coming to know in science perhaps because it leans so heavily on the empirical. Indeed, the focus on empirical data and the differences in the way that data are treated in science and religion account largely for what is perceived as the dichotomy between the two realms. However, our examination of the routes to being would not be complete without consideration of the scientific pattern finder.

For the pattern finder, being is found in shape and number. The procedure followed is to sift through the data searching for vaguely defined regularities of a geometric or numerical kind on the basis of a faith that such regularities must exist and need merely to be uncovered. Such an attitude is very much in the tradition of Pythagoras. Philolaus, one of the Pythagoreans, is supposed to have written:

> The nature of number is to be a standard of reference, of guidance, and of instruction in every doubt and difficulty. Were it not for number, nothing that exists would be clear to anybody either in itself or in its relation to other things.[3]

The connection between number and being took on a distinctly religious and mystical tone. Quoting Philolaus again:

> Consider the effects and the nature of number according to the power that resides in the Decad [see Fig. 8.2]. It is great, all-powerful, all-sufficing, the first principle and guide in the life of Gods, of Heaven, of Men. Without it all is with-

out limit, obscure, indiscernible. . . . One can observe the power of number exercising itself not only in the affairs of demons and of gods, but in all the acts and thoughts of men. . . . [4]

$$
\begin{array}{ccccc}
 & & 1 & & = 1 \\
 & 1 & 1 & & = 2 \\
1 & 1 & 1 & & = 3 \\
1 & 1 & 1 & 1 & = \underline{4} \\
 & & & & 10
\end{array}
$$

Fig. 8.2 The Pythagorean representation of the Decad, as a triangular number.

Casper and Noer in their book, *Revolutions in Physics* (1972), go on to say that "The properties of numbers were studied by the Pythagoreans in much the same spirit in which Christian monks later studied the Scriptures."[5]

The same mind-set can be understood to pervade those who looked at the heavens and described their aspects in geometrical terms. To find the pattern was to find the expression of the gods. The scientist today who seeks the shape or number that will unify the observations will, upon discovering such a unity, believe not that the voice of the gods has been heard but rather that what is real, what truly exists, or as we might say, being itself has been uncovered.

The pattern finder in science can be seen to fall between the worker in a state of second naïveté who applies theoretical understandings without questioning them and the metaphor maker who distorts the world of meanings. Johannes Kepler worked with Tycho Brahe's positions of the planet Mars, trying to find a mathematical description of the motion. Kepler, who had earlier thought that the five perfect solids could explain the number and arrangement of the planets in the solar system, epitomizes the Pythagorean pattern finder. He stands between Brahe, who in some ways can be understood to have operated at the level of second naïveté, and Isaac Newton, the metaphor maker *par excellence*, who insisted that the mechanical rules or laws that

Galileo applied to the terrestrial world were the same rules or laws that accounted for the behavior of the objects that populate the heavens. Newton's metaphorical act made the laws of earth the same as the laws of heaven.

The work of the Pythagoreans goes on today. When Werner Heisenberg in 1925 proposed that the states of atoms could be expressed as an array of numbers (Fig. 8.3a), he was giving expression to an understanding of microscopic matter in a way that would have delighted Pythagoras. When Murray Gell-Mann, in 1963, proposed a symmetrical arrangement of elementary particles in a form he called the Eightfold Way, based on the special unitary group in three dimensions, he was putting forth a found pattern, a triangular array of numbers (Fig. 8.3b), that seemed to him to represent the way things were at the submicroscopic level. The symbol at the top of Gell-Mann's array corresponds to a particle that had never been observed, a particle Gell-Mann named the Omega Minus. One can imagine the degree to which the sense of the reality of the pattern was reinforced when some months later a new particle was found that had the properties predicted for the Omega Minus.

$$\frac{1}{2}\hbar \begin{bmatrix} 3 & 0 & 0 & 0 \\ 0 & 1 & 0 & 0 \\ 0 & 0 & -1 & 0 \\ 0 & 0 & 0 & -3 \end{bmatrix}$$

(a)

$$\Omega^-$$
$$\Xi^{*-} \quad \Xi^{*\circ}$$
$$\Sigma^{*-} \quad \Sigma^{*\circ} \quad \Sigma^{*+}$$
(b) $\Delta^- \quad \Delta^\circ \quad \Delta^+ \quad \Delta^{++}$

Fig. 8.3 Pythagorean-like representations of characteristics of particles in atomic and elementary particle physics: (a) a Heisenberg angular momentum matrix, (b) Gell-Mann's arrangement of the heavy particles according to their charge, hypercharge, and mass.

Since the ontological status of the elementary particles is today still very much in doubt, they can hardly be said to be understood at the level of second naïveté. It is not correct, therefore, to call Gell-Mann's work hypothetico-deductive even though it seems to have some of the characteristics of the theoretical methodologies that are used in the process of filling the gaps, nor can it be said to represent an example of metaphor making. The physics of particles appears still to await the grand synthesis that is achieved in the metaphoric act.

The four routes to being are now seen to be traversed by four kinds of persons. The person of first naïveté has a fixed world of meanings that is related to the self. The person of second naïveté works in terms of established theories and enlarges the world of meanings by filling in the gaps. The pattern maker questions the established theories and sifts through the empirical data searching for patterns that will push out the horizons of our world of meanings. Finally, the person who reaches a point of vantage from which it becomes possible to reshape the world of meanings by metaphoric distortion transcends the level of second naïveté and the world of meanings itself.

Whichever route to being we might consider, it is the ontological flash that creates the sense of presence before that which is. What finally, then, is an ontological flash? An ontological flash is an event which creates conviction. Such an event explodes conceptual horizons: it occurs in the realm of limit-question (in Tracy's sense) and involves what Ramsey called a disclosure. These moments of insight carry conviction precisely because they are limit-experiences. They instill a sense of completion, of perfection, and of beauty that prevents question.

We have all had our share of such experiences. They sometimes come in the form of what might be called an ontological crisis. When you back your new car forcefully into a telephone pole and get out to look at the damage, there is no doubt, as much as you might wish to doubt. The situation, as it appears, is the way that it is.

THE "ONTOLOGICAL FLASH" IN RELIGIOUS METAPHOR

One of the oldest philosophical truths is ontological in its referent: being, according to Aristotle, is said in many ways. Since Aristotle, the question of being has been itself reformulated in multiple ways. Up until this century the status of the question was often disputed. Being and becoming were set over and against each other as antinomies, and philosophers were often labeled according to which category seemed to be central to their conception of reality.

The question of being is implicit, if only in its naïve form, whenever we reflect on the status of objects. Suppose we have before us a small flat round pebble. Under what conditions might we claim that this stone is real? Someone might call attention to its weight, size, and the elements of which is appears to be made. Someone else might remark that the pebble, along with others, used to constitute the beach upon which it was "discovered." Still another person might observe that the pebble could be used for skimming or "skipping" across the water. In short, any common-sense claims pertaining to the reality of the stone would probably be based on the pebble's constitution, on the context of its appearance, and on its function. Under what conditions might we claim the stone to be "unreal"? Someone might say that the pebble appeared in the middle of her dream last night; another that it followed him around the table. Still another person might claim that little people live in the stone. All of these considerations involve reflections on the context of appearance, function and constitution of an object. In other words, the reality or non-reality of the pebble is determined by its being understood by way of shared and communicable criteria for reality.

Suppose that next to the pebble is a violin. What are the conditions under which we would be willing to claim that it is a "real" violin? We might say that we own it and that we play it. We may add that so far as we know its history, the violin has been constituted in such a way that the instrument sings sweetly or raucously, depending on how it is bowed. What are the conditions under which we would be apt to claim that it is not a "real" violin? If it began breathing, or if it were suddenly revealed to be made of chocolate, or if it sounded like a trumpet, someone could be expected to exclaim, "It looks like a violin but it can't be a real one!"

Say that in a certain university classroom one has a form of liberal arts education. Do the same general criteria for the existence of education apply? Can we talk about the constitution and

appearance of the liberal arts, their use and function, the context of their appearance? In what sense can a liberal arts education be said to "exist" in a college or university?

All three of these examples—the beings of pebble, violin, and
liberal arts education—show that even in our everyday commerce, questions about being arise. In their most unreflective
and naïve form, ontological questions are concerned with the
status of beings in our worlds of meanings. Although philosophy
gives us the clearest distinctions, poetry sometimes is better able
to disclose the limit-character of these ontological questions: our
inability to give comprehensive, as distinct from partial, answers. In the following poem, "Ontology," by Howard McCord,
the ontological flash is cast in a seductively negative light:

Very little exists.
Chicago, for example,
does not exist.
I have seen it twice
and there is nothing there.
It does not even have a history.

Grasshoppers do not exist
either.
Minute examination
reveals them as small
webs of colored light,
vibrating like stars.
Nothing more.

Old texts say
a few trees exist,
but they are so deeply
hidden in the woods
that is is unlikely
any will be discovered
in our day.[6]

By denying those aspects of existence of familiar objects that we are non-reflectively most sure of, the poem teases us into the question of existence.

In our naïve discourse about beings in the world, we ourselves assume a way of being wherein we self-consciously reflect on modes of being. Self-consciousness is the condition for the possibility of a critical ontology. As far as we know, only human beings ask the question of "being." Even if we fail to ask the question of being, assumptions about being can be seen to underlie every one of our questions. Martin Heidegger began his major work, *Being and Time* (1927), with the complaint, "This question [of being] has today been forgotten."[7] Heidegger, however, unnecessarily dichotomized science and philosophy. He thought that science was "anti-ontological" because it systematically ignored the question of being.

The word "ontology" has a revealing etymology. It comes from the Greek word "ontos" which is a form of the verb "to be" and "logos" which is a form of the verb "to know." Understood by way of these verb forms, the word ontology takes on an active sense: following Heidegger, we can say ontology is knowing about the ways things manifest themselves in the totality of their existence. In classical philosophy, however, the word "ontology" often had a conclusivist sense: "ontos" was understood as "essence" and "logos" was understood as "knowledge of." And so ontology took on a passive quality: it denoted the way things are in the sense of fate or predestination. Because of their rejections of the classical sense of ontology, some contemporary philosophers and theologians continue to oppose the use of the term. Others attempt to retrieve and reformulate the sense of the word in the light of contemporary issues and problems. Heidegger, for example, redefined the meaning of "human" in an explicitly ontological sense by using the word *Dasein*: *Dasein* means the "there-being of the question of being."[8] Where else, in other words, except in the location of the human, is the question of being to be found?

Can things be and not be at the same time? For thinkers of antiquity they could not. The classical Greek philosophers, for example, restricted their understanding of existence in accordance with the principle of contradiction: a thing can't be A and not A at the same time. But Hegel, in the early nineteenth century, tried in several ways to clarify the dialectical character of all understanding and ultimately of being itself. As soon as we think of being, he thought, it is always with respect to something that is determinate.[9] In other words, nothing exists without its being immersed in the struggle for determination. If something were not involved in that struggle, it would be nothing.

Hegel built his concept of the dialectical character of understanding on the foregoing assumption of determination. He suggested two ways in which determinate being is involved in self-contradiction. First, something is what it is by being in contrast to something else. This is true in the order of being as well as in the order of knowing. Hegel gave an example in which the order of being is analogous to the order of knowing. A meadow exists by contrast with a wood and a pond. A meadow, then, is defined in the order of knowing by being contrasted with a wood and a pond and in relation to them. In a sense, meadow is the "other" of wood and pond. Here we see that something is what it is by being the "other" of some determinate others.

Second, something is what it is by interacting with something else. Hegel's example of a meadow here, taken in the order of being, is analogous to a meadow in the order of knowing. Imagine that over the years, a meadow could be transformed into a wood or a pond, if the wind blew seeds which grew into trees upon it or if sufficient water drained into it. A meadow, then, is what it is by maintaining itself against becoming a wood or a pond. In this sense, a meadow is what it is not only in itself but also in relation to determinate others. Then we can say that what a meadow is has within it its interactions with what it is not. Through this analogy, we can say that the understanding contains within itself its own negation, since it contains within itself that which is and is not.[10]

By giving several accounts of the dialectical character of understanding, Hegel showed that "not A" reveals itself after all to be "A."[11] His point was not that games are being played with classical logic but that in the actual movement of thought from immediacy to mediateness, we glimpse that intrinsic relationship between thinking and being as a dynamic process distinct from a static, given reality.

If conceived of within a naïve ontology, objects—a pebble, a violin, a liberal arts education—are likely to be construed as bodies rather than as things because they will appear to be already-out-there-now-real. In contrast with these earlier examples, the following examples, taken from Hindu and Christian scriptures and neo-orthodox and revisionist theologies, are more abstract and difficult to construe as bodies. As these latter examples more easily lend themselves to analysis as things, they suggest that the demand for a critical ontology extends to the earlier examples as well.

If we understand ontology as the work of presencing, that is, of making explicit the way things manifest themselves in their total existence, we can expect perceptible differences in the ontologies of humans as expressed in their religions and theologies. Let us examine two classical religious texts, one Hindu and one Judaic and Christian.

First a story from the Upanishad:

Now there was Shvetaketu Aruneya. To him his father said: "That which is the finest essence—this whole world has that as its soul. That is Reality. That is Atman. That art thou, Shvetaketu."

"Do you, Sir, cause me to understand even more."
"So be it, my dear," said he. . . . "Bring hither a fig."
"Here it is, Sir."
"Divide it."
"It is divided, Sir."
"What do you see there?"
"Those rather fine seeds, Sir."
"Of these, please divide one."
"It is divided, Sir."
"What do you see there?"
"Nothing at all, Sir."

Then he said to him: "Verily, my dear, that finest essence which you do not perceive—verily, my dear, from that finest essence this great Nyagrodha (sacred fig) tree thus arises. Believe me, my dear," said he, "that which is the finest essence—this whole world has that as its soul. That is Reality. That is Atman. That art thou, Shvetaketu."[12]

In this story the question of being is already explicit. The story begins with an assertion regarding the "essence" of the world. The speaker, by means of the assertion, forges an identity between the world and the listener, his son. But no information is given regarding the "nature" of identity. Then follows a stichometrical exchange which, by example, dramatizes for us once again the inadequacy of the sense-perception model of experience for knowing about the "essence" of the world. The story concludes with a reassertion of the premise of the initial dialogue, this time stated as a conclusion to the example.

We notice that the emphasis here rests on the strength of the assertion, rather than on any attempt at argument. The example is a negative reinforcement of the premise. In Hindu philosophy, essence is elaborated in relation to consciousness: pure consciousness comes into full being when the soul is sleeplessly intent. This is further interpreted as "pure intuitional consciousness, where there is no knowledge of objects internal or external."[13]

Some commentators have pointed out that the strong and explicit antipathy to matter may reflect the basic "unfriendliness" of the land and climate of South Asia toward its population. Irrespective of its multi-faceted origin, the effect of this aversion to "matter" is to dispose one toward a transcendent state of consciousness—state of being—which is characterized by luminousness and tranquillity.

Next is a story from the Christian Testament.

Then the disciples went up to him and asked, "Why do you talk to them in parables?" "Because," he replied, "the mysteries of the kingdom of heaven are revealed to you, but they are not revealed to them. For anyone who has will be given more, and he will have more than enough;

but from anyone who has not, even what he
has will be taken away. The reason I talk
to them in parables is that they look
without seeing and listen without hearing
or understanding. So in their case this
prophecy of Isaiah is being fulfilled:
You will listen again, but not understand,
see and see again, but not perceive.
For the heart of this nation has grown
coarse, their ears are dull of hearing, and
they have shut their eyes, for fear they
should see with their eyes,
hear with their ears,
understand with their heart,
and be converted
and be healed by me.
But happy are your eyes because they see,
your ears because they hear! I tell you
solemnly, many prophets and old men longed
to see what you see, and never saw it; to
hear what you hear, and never heard it.[14]

On one level, the question of being in this passage is implicit in
the central image of the "kingdom of heaven," which transposes
the meaning of "having," "seeing," "hearing," and "understanding" from experience understood on the model of sense perception to experience understood as self-transcendence. The
passage begins with a question regarding the way mysteries are
revealed: that is, by the use of parables rather than "plain
speech." The speaker (Jesus) confirms that the hearers (disciples)
have received the revelation. Strictly speaking, no information
is given regarding the "nature" of the Kingdom. There follows a
quotation from Isaiah the prophet, recalling the social context of
the originating religious expression in the Hebrew testament.
The passage concludes by reminding the hearers of their own situation—that they do see and do hear and that others have
longed for what they see and hear but have not found it.

On a second level, the question of being is to be found in the curious secretiveness of the kingdom. An interesting complication ensues once the words quoted in a parable become a written text. The words pertaining to whoever has received the revelation directly, without parable, are presumably directed to the disciples of Jesus, his first audience. All others—the "them" to whom the mysteries of the kingdom have not been revealed— are given parables. Once a parable itself is written and narrated in a larger context, the entire text constitutes both the mystery and its revelation, at once the secret and its disclosure for anyone who reads.

In this scriptural text, the emphasis falls upon the mode of participation in the revelation, that is, all those activities—seeing, hearing, understanding with the heart, being converted, being healed—associated with "having" the revelation. Whereas in the Hindu text the state of identity ("That Is Reality; that is Atman. That art thou, . . .") is the primary focus, the action of participation and reception (" . . . happy are your eyes because they see, your ears because they hear!") is the key to the Judaic and Christian texts. Whereas there is an atemporal quality about the Hindu text (" . . . the whole world has that as its soul"), there is evidence of an historical consciousness in the Christian text ("So in their case this prophecy of Isaiah is being fulfilled . . . many . . . have longed to see what you see"). Despite the risk of drawing conclusions based on a comparison of only two texts, it is apparent that the ontologies of these two texts are distinct.

Distinctions between ontologies can be found in representative theologies as well as in different religions. Neo-orthodox theology which informed much of post-World War I critical thought, for example, reflected a disillusion with the world and an emphasis on the kind of faith that goes contrary to appearances and sets itself over and against any other kinds of claims to know reality. Neo-orthodox theologies exhibited a heightened sense of the negativities of existence and of the untrustworthiness of human experience. Whereas the liberal and modernist theologies, which preceded the neo-orthodox, emphasized the likeness of the sacred and the human in the figure of Jesus, neo-orthodox theology became distinguished for its distancing of the sacred from the human in the concept of God as "qualitatively different" from anything that is human.

Revisionist theology, in its reflection on the "way things are," includes the emphasis of both liberal and neo-orthodox theology: a basic trust and confidence in human experience and a recognition of limitations and possible reversals. Insisting on fundamental differences between religious faith and superficial optimism, revisionist theology looks to other perspectives—the sociological, the psychological, that of the physical sciences—as well as that of the religious to contribute to theological understanding. In this way it shows explicit confidence in the human ability to know, albeit not exhaustively, and holds that that public discourse among people of differing points of view is necessary. Its ontology is discernible in concepts such as that of a dipolar God who is both changing and stable, excelling in godliness yet relating to humankind.

Understood as metaphoric, religious ontologies can be seen for what they most centrally are: comprehensive insistences that being human in the world is or is to be an integrative experience surpassing all other ways of being which oppose or threaten this final, more than merely human, ambition. In established religious traditions, metaphors are embedded in the basic terms of canonical writings, the genres of which "preserve" originating metaphors, for example, God-with-us. Metaphors also arrive on the scene in new forms, insights which "reveal" the way things are in the contemporary situation, for example, the god-is-dead of Nietzsche. That which is intrinsic to the metaphor, namely, the insistence (in the face of resistance) that what the metaphoric insight discloses is the way things are is perhaps most clearly seen in the prophetic statements of any age.

Understood as metaphoric, theological ontologies also take on a vital role in human understanding: theology creates new metaphors to retrieve and restore tension to the original root-metaphors for a given generation. David Tracy's metaphor of "Jesus as the Supreme Fiction" exemplifies this task.[15] The truth here insisted upon is the indispensibility of imagination in the task of accounting for both fiction in general and the Christian religious tradition, replete with all its expressiveness. Tracy is persuaded that Jesus can be a decisive (although not necessarily exclusive) representation of God for anyone who can understand in terms of "a supreme fiction." Neither Tracy's nor Nietzsche's metaphors are exclusive of others well known to the Christian tradition.

What is the metaphoric process in "Jesus as the Supreme Fiction"? First, and most obviously, the Christian understanding of Jesus from the field of religion and the contemporary understanding of fiction from the field of literary criticism are forced together. The resulting clash challenges both fundamentalist Christian and "purely" aesthetic understandings of the way things are. No longer is fiction "merely" a story; it is a process which opens new possible worlds and new possibilities of being in those worlds. No longer is Jesus merely an historical person, but also, as in Wallace Stevens' poem, "Notes Toward a Supreme Fiction" (from which one part of the metaphor is derived), something which by necessity includes aspects of abstraction, change, and pleasure:

> It is possible, possible, possible. It must
> Be possible. It must be that in time
> The real will from its crude compoundings come,
>
> Seeming, at first, a beast disgorged, unlike,
> Warmed by a desperate milk. To find the real,
> To be stripped of every fiction except one,
>
> The fiction of an absolute . . . [16]

The metaphoric process that puts the two fields of meaning (fiction in literary criticism, God in theology) together creates a tension of sustained inquiry—a tension which is preserved by the ontological conviction that the new meaning carries.

The metaphoric aspect of this new christological model can be seen also in the revisionist theologian's insistence that the best of liberal and neo-orthodox modes of religious thought, ordinarily at odds with each other, be conjoined. The liberal position by itself maintains that different fields of inquiry should be brought to bear on the Christian reality; the neo-orthodox by itself maintains that the qualitative difference between the human and the sacred should be the basis of theological understanding. The metaphor "Jesus as the Supreme Fiction," as an example of the work of revisionist theology, illustrates how the metaphoric act not only produces a distortion in the fields as originally constituted but also creates newly conceived possible ways of being and understanding.

CHAPTER NINE

Truths and Theories

T HE PROLOGUES are over. It is a question, now,
Of final belief. So, say that final belief
Must be in a fiction. It is time to choose.[1]

Until now we have postponed the questions of adequacy and
appropriateness. Here we discover that our first loyalty is to a
larger truth than that with which we first began. Then is there
no truth without theory? This chapter attempts to address that
question.

A SYNTHESIS: HORIZON-GROWTH IN NATURAL
PHILOSOPHY AND RELIGION

Our belief in the existence of a common basis underlying the
"quests for truth" that go on within theology and natural philosophy is grounded in the fact that these quests are all human quests
for understanding and that the common nature of being human
provides sufficient warrant for our search for this common basis.
It follows from the "commonness" of this foundation that, to the
extent that we have been able to find it, the foundation should
be explicable without regard to either theology or natural philosophy. At the basic level the objective is seen not as an understanding of this or that but as a quest for understanding itself
and, in particular, for the elements, structures, relations, and
limitations that are characteristic of human understandings generally. Let us then attempt a synthesis of the cognitive elements
which we have called into play in the past eight chapters.

Our first task in this construction is to distinguish between
knowledge and understanding, a distinction made difficult be-

cause much common usage of the term "knowing" includes understanding as well as other cognitive states such as awareness
and recognition. However, for our purposes we need to differentiate these concepts and will do this by means of a taxonomy that
includes both. This taxonomy recognizes six distinct cognitive
levels: ignorance, acquaintance (or recognition), appreciation
(or valuing), knowledge (the functional level), understanding
(the level of meaning), and comprehension (the universal level).
The outstanding characteristic of this sequence is that each
state, beginning with appreciation, presupposes the one that pre-
cedes it. In addition it is possible for us to apply the lower cognitive states to bodies, the intermediate ones to either bodies or
things, while the upper states appear to be restricted to things
alone. We now apply our terminology about cognition (what we
think) to our ontology (what there is).

Ludwig Wittgenstein, in his *Tractatus* and other writings,
spoke of "states of affairs."[2] For example he said, "A state of affairs [a state of things] is a combination of objects [things]" and
"In a state of affairs objects stand in a determinate relation to one
another."[3] It is useful to think of a state of affairs as made up of
things and relations among things. It is also important to notice
that the relations among things are themselves things, that these
latter things (that is, relations) can be related to each other, and
that, furthermore, the relations among relations are also things,
etc. To know a state of affairs is to know the objects that go to
make up the state of affairs. This is to say that the objects in the
state of affairs can be recognized, appreciated, and can in some
sense be "used." There can, of course, be degrees of completeness
in the knowledge that one can have of a state of affairs.

What then does it mean to say that one understands a state of
affairs? To understand a state of affairs is to know the things that
go to make it up: that is, to know the objects and the relations
among the objects (and among the relations as well). Again, one
is not restricted here either to no understanding on the one hand
or complete understanding on the other. An understanding of a
state of affairs can be partial.

It is possible, of course, to be in a situation in which one can
know more than one can say (or express). In fact it could be the

case, depending upon one's ability to express what one knows, that one could know much more than one can express. It is also possible to understand more than one can express. That is to say that it is possible to know the relations among the objects in a state of affairs and not be able to describe or explain these relations to another person.

It must be true that some of the great leaders throughout early history had understandings of states of affairs that made it possible for them to govern effectively or to do battle brilliantly. However, from the performance of their successors it is apparent that the understandings of genius died with the genius. Now it may be true that the understandings were jealously kept secret lest the leader be overthrown. But in at least some of these cases, we may conclude that the leader who was so effective in conceiving and carrying out plans was unable to communicate the basic understandings for doing this to subordinates or successors. At least as important, then, as the search for human understandings is the search for the means of communicating those understandings. It is not at all surprising to find metaphor on the front lines of this struggle. We will shortly return to a further analysis of the situation that is the case when one's understanding is inexpressible. But first, just what is an expressed understanding?

We might first ask what it means to express knowledge of a state of affairs. According to our usage the expression of knowledge of a state of affairs corresponds to a communication regarding the objects and perhaps some of the relations in the state of affairs. A description of an historic situation, for example, would constitute such an expression. However, there is no specific focus on relations in the expression of knowledge of a state of affairs. What does it mean then to express an understanding of a state of affairs? Again we can apply our use of understanding and say that to express an understanding is to express the relations that are the case with respect to objects and other relations within a state of affairs. Now there is something peculiarly abstract about the expression of relations in the absence of a concomitant expression of the objects. It is perfectly possible to understand that an expression of relations would hold for a great many states of affairs that differ only with respect to the objects that populate them. In other words there is, in an expression of relations or in the expression of an understanding, an inherent generality not present in an expression of knowledge. This general expression of understanding, this expression of relations without specification of the particular objects which are related is what we call theory. It is to this idea of theory that we now turn our attention.

The minimal requirements of a theory are that it possess coherence on the one hand and correspondence on the other. Coherence relates to the fact that a theory refers to some part or all of a state of affairs or a related set of states of affairs. A theory does not possess coherence if part of it relates to one state of affairs and part of it relates to another, otherwise unrelated state of affairs. A theory is also noncoherent if it contains "logical" gaps, by which we mean that it contains two or more groups of relations that are not themselves related.

An examination of the correspondence of a theory is involved when one asks about the objects to which the theory applies. If these objects cannot be found to exist, the theory lacks correspondence. However, we do not claim that any objects exist in the absence of the theory, merely that they exist in relation to the theory. This approach avoids slipping into a body-oriented objectivism. It is also important to remember that there is no requirement that specific objects exist in correspondence with the theory. Such a requirement would destroy the generality that we said was inherent in the theory's relational character.

At the beginning we were exploring the structure of human quests for understanding, what Hanson called the goal of intelligibility. We identified these quests for understanding with "quests for truth." Truth, then, becomes inextricably bound up with understanding just as understanding, as expressed, is inextricably bound up with theory. This is not to say that all theories are true, or that all understandings are satisfactory to our demands for intelligibility merely on the basis of their own structure. To examine this final question of the truth of a theory we must move away from the object pole of the human-world interaction and closer to the subject pole. We must examine the need for judgments of validation and verification.

Let us presume the existence of a theory that is said to apply to a variety of states of affairs. If I know the theory I know the relations among the things in any of these states of affairs and I understand these states of affairs. I do understand, that is, if I make valid use of the theory. If I posit an object in an appropriate state of affairs, I can claim validity for a conclusion only if the relations have been properly traversed. Theory itself, even the best available theory, is not proof against its mistaken application. We ask ourselves now if the valid conclusion corresponds to our experience. If it does, our confidence in the intelligibility of our world is increased.

Although this is our own world, we do not live in our world alone. And so we now ask whether our understanding increases the intelligibility of our world as the world for and of others? If it does not, those others become less intelligible to us, which in turn reduces the intelligibility of our world (since the others are contained in our world). If on the other hand, our understanding of our world increases the intelligibility of our world as the world for and of others, then our own world is even better understood by ourselves. The test for an intersubjective increase in intelligibility is what we have been calling verification. Here we have asked of another, "Does this valid conclusion—valid according to my theory—correspond to your experience? In particular, does it correspond to your experience understood in the light of my theory?" In all of this there is no great difficulty because the theory is an expressed understanding. And this brings us back to the most difficult situation which we set aside earlier and forces us to ask, "What can be said about those understandings which we cannot express?"

We are now back to the case of the individual who is in possession of an understanding of certain states of affairs but who, for one reason or another, is unable to express this understanding. Two possibilities seem to exist here. The first is that the understanding can somehow be transmitted to another without the expression of understanding as theory. We will examine this further in a moment. The second possibility is that the understanding remains private. Our first question is whether we can calm validity for any conclusion based on private understanding. To this we must answer, no. Without the expression of theory we would seem to have no way to determine error. The resort to experience cannot distinguish incorrect understanding from the incorrect application of a correct understanding. This is not to say that the understanding is useless. Far from it. The understanding could be of very great value in living in the world. Under these circumstances one's obligation might be to search for a means of expression. Clearly, it is important to develop new ways of communicating understandings. Indeed, such activity may be just as vital as the development of the understandings themselves.

We return now to our first possibility of communicating or perhaps simply transferring an inexpressible understanding from one person to another. Perhaps one can "grow" an understanding in another person. The growth that takes place in this way would most likely be related to shared or common experiences. In these cases verification is possible even in the absence of validation. And here the tests of increased intelligibility might be understood to operate on a collective level. The danger lies in the possibility of a false understanding increasing the intelligibility of the world merely because the understanding is commonly held.

We have, then, if only in the most sketchy way, explicated the common basis that underlies the human quests for understanding. We have, furthermore, pointed out the essential role that theory must play in these endless searches. We are, at this point, left in an unfortunate position with respect to our objectives regarding religion and science, or more properly, theology and natural philosophy. We are in possession of an epistemological structure that, while common to both disciplines, could nonetheless relate to two entirely different worlds. What provides for the amalgamation of these worlds? What aspect of the quests for understanding in theology and natural philosophy makes these two worlds one?

The answer is found not in the understandings themselves but rather in the way in which the understandings come into being. The natural philosopher or theologian, in coming to know, encounters a limit-situation, experiences an ontological flash, has a disclosure experience, and in so doing, engages that which is entirely other. Here no doubt is possible. At this moment there is a conviction, a sense of certainty that is not justified by any formal epistemological structure. Validation and verification come later as the new knowledge is tested and takes its place within our structure of understanding the world. But at that moment it is given.

It is the commonness of that other, encountered in limit-experience, that makes the world of theology and the world of natural philosophy one world.

A MEDIATION: HORIZON-GROWTH IN PHILOSOPHY OF RELIGION AND SCIENCE

What does the metaphoric process as we understand it enable us to say about the relationship of science and religion which we could not say before? When we have said all that we can about that relationship, what is the extent to which we have commented on human knowing in general? In other words, what do we know when our worlds of meanings include both the scientific and the religious fields of meanings? To answer these questions, we trace what happens to the metaphoric act from its moment of inception: how it is formulated in expression, extended in communication, and related to knowledge-in-process.

Our understanding of the metaphoric process, like that of knowledge-in-process, begins with this premise: In encountering the world, we constitute it. That is, on the level of experience a certain pattern of the way of being human begins to assert itself. We dimly perceive limits to that pattern as well, and these perceptions, if heightened in peculiar moments of self-awareness, are capable of expression. We have called these awarenesses limit-experiences. To perceive the truth of our starting-point— that in encountering the world, we constitute it—is to recognize that there is a human pattern and to know also that there are limits to that pattern. The metaphoric process on the level of experience, then, elicits a sudden new specification of being. The world of meanings, our epistemic world, is distorted; that is, it suffers a torque or warping of ordinary meanings.

Once at the level of understanding, metaphor as a new specification of being is found in all forms of communication: it may appear as artistic, scientific, mathematical, or social. No formula exists either to generate a successful metaphor or to translate it successfully into another modality. As ontological, metaphor is also a limit-expression.

Once at the level of judgment, this new meaning as communicated is on its way to becoming public. Shared, the distortion is intersubjectively known and is thereby capable of verification. Affirmed, substantiated by the experience and understanding of others, it may even give rise to limit-concepts. Insofar as limit-concepts are public, they subsist discursively in the collaboration of those who have understood the metaphoric process together.

Finally, the metaphor is reconstituted when we re-encounter it. In re-encountering something, we are in a sense not the same individuals who encountered it in the first instance. Our experience of commonality, for example—our sense of being a self in a world with others—transcends our sense of ourselves as private. Once we have had the experience of cooperative activity, we know that some understandings are accessible only collaboratively. Similarly, the ontological world and its intelligibility are a world's difference from the existential notion that there are only selves and others.

But a new theoretical basis for viewing the world is not, in itself, enough. The world must be constructed in such a way as to have the possibility of containing those objects and relations essential to the theoretical framework. There is a necessary circularity in this statement. The world must be furnished with an adequate ontology, specifically an ontology that makes explicit the role of conscious human beings. Prevailing ontologies tend to overemphasize the Cartesian world of natural philosophy which does not include conscious human beings, and so there is no possibility for intersubjectivity, for verification, for truths held in common. Moreover, such a world contains knowledge only in the sense of public knowledge as in Holton's public science, so that knowledge-in-process with its disclosures, its ontological flashes and its limit-experiences is excluded. Accordingly, we must make our ontology explicit if it is to serve the needs of our understanding.

Toward a New Ontology

In Cartesian ontology, one looks out at a world that contains many objects that have a wide variety of physical properties and behaviors. Included among these objects are certain ones which might be called "boxes" with "two holes" that investigation shows receive a variety of sensory signals from their surroundings. It is interesting that these boxes have a less broad spectrum of physical properties than do the other objects; in other words, they seem to be physically similar. However, they show a much wider spectrum of behavior. Everything (including all these boxes) that is seen (or smelled, heard, etc.) out there is the world encountered at an initial moment of consciousness, a world that stands over and apart from the self which is in here looking out—through two holes. All that there is can be understood to be out there with those other things or in here with the self.

Such is the common-sense view, oversimplified perhaps and starkly presented for the sake of clarity. But although this view is generally discredited by modern philosophers, efforts to generate a new understanding, to formulate a more effective ontology have not moved smoothly from this Cartesian view in such a way as to show just what is at stake, what changes need to be made, and how these changes can be effected.

In our revised ontology, humans interact with their environment by some adaptive processes so that created in them is a structure that enables them to impose patterns on their world. Up to this point we are in agreement with Hanson and Kuhn. At this point, however, we depart from them in two significant ways—one which refines and one which enlarges the ontology that gives rise to our epistemological position which encompasses both science and religion.

By way of refinement, we incorporate Lonergan's distinction between bodies (objects which relate only to ourselves) and things (objects which relate to other objects), and we show that the theory-laden character of experience can be distinguished from the naïve understanding of immediate experience. This distinction allows us to avoid the "all or nothing" position that Hanson fell into when he wrote, for example, that *all* "seeing" is "seeing as," that is, that all experience is theory-laden. With the distinction between things and bodies (that is, between the theoretical understanding of experience as relation and the naïve understanding of immediate experience), we can claim that at one level of experience Tycho Brahe and Johannes Kepler "saw" the same object as body, namely, the sun rising above the horizon at dawn. The difficulty with Hanson's view is that he had no way to rescue theory from getting lost in the unconscious. When Kepler and Brahe were seeing the same thing, that seeing was devoid of theory. However, when Hanson said that they saw different things, theory was there unconsciously and he had no way of making theory explicit. Only by treating theory systematically as a conscious cognitive structure can we develop an epistemological model which includes a world of meanings and a field of meanings and that incorporates the many acts of knowing we have described earlier.

By way of enlargement, we use Rahner's conception of the relationships that exist between self and other in such a way as to make possible a world that is much larger than the Cartesian world that restricts the cognitive processes to routine scientific activity and deductive theological speculation. This enlarged world includes the self as object and results in a transformation that makes possible the development of concepts, such as limit-experience, in such a way as to clarify the place of revelation, disclosure, the ontological flash, in knowledge-in-process in both religion and science.

What is conspicuous about this larger world that includes the self? When the edge of a mirror is placed on the ground in front of an animal, the animal, if it pays any attention at all, can be expected to stare and then perhaps to look around behind the mirror. After repeated exploratory moves, the animal will soon lose interest in the mirror and its image and pay no more attention to it. What can be surmised from this loss of interest?

The animal sees the image—an object in the Cartesian sense —and responds to it as if it were an animate body, an already-out-there-now-real. However, further investigation makes it clear that this object does not, for example, smell like another animal. It therefore is not an animal or anything else of interest. We think we can safely assume that after investigation the object seen by the animal in no way, for the animal, constitutes a representation of an animal.

The animal's behavior differs from that of the classical figure of Narcissus. In the myth of Narcissus, a boy falls hopelessly in love with the person whose image he sees reflected in a pool. Narcissus' response was much different from the response of the animal. Narcissus knew immediately and without further investigation that the image he saw was the image of a person. Narcissus did not know (we will assume this for the purpose of our argument) that the person whose image he saw was himself. In other words he saw other persons out there in the world and could recognize images of persons as relating to persons out there in the world. But he did not see this particular image as relating to himself. Narcissus lacked the kind of self-awareness of which we now wish to speak.

In our world, larger than the Cartesian world, when I "look at" the world I "see" myself in it. That is, when I reflect on what the world is, the world that I reflect on, which is still the world as experienced, contains myself. I am in the world. This is what is meant by saying that one has self-awareness. This now brings us back to the central thesis of this chapter. It will be argued here that something very special occurs when this self-awareness manifests itself.

When I see myself in the world I see my self as aware that I see myself. That is, one's self-awareness is part of the world. This state of affairs radically alters the dimensions of existence in the world. We explain by way of an analogy.

When one looks at a picture one sees an object that presents, in two dimensions, what is usually understood to have three. That is, the objects portrayed are expected (with rare exceptions) to be thought of as three-dimensional objects arranged in

a more or less Cartesian three-dimensional space with fore-
ground and background. But the situation is radically altered
when the picture contains itself, that is, when the picture one is
looking at is included in the picture as one of the objects pic-
tured. When this happens an entirely new dimension of non-
Cartesian depth springs into existence, and one can see picture
after picture after picture as one looks more and more closely.
This, we argue, is exactly parallel to the transformation that
takes place when we see the world as containing our self-aware
self. Our awareness of the world becomes part of the world of
which we are aware.

The introduction of self-aware objects into the world results in
our being able to experience as objects, things we know to be
subjects. And conversely, all objects experienced in the world
can be understood to be a part of the subjects who experience
them. When, for example, I consider myself in the world as
aware of some object, that object appears as an awareness of a
subject which in turn reminds me that the object itself in the
world is an object experienced by me, the one who is considering
the world.

We can now see that self-awareness generates an objectivity at
a higher level than the objectivity of Cartesian dualism. For the
inclusion of my self-aware self in the world raises the question of
the difference between myself in the world and the other objects
in the world. With self-awareness (of the kind Narcissus lacked)
we can distinguish the other objects in the world, including
other humans, from ourselves.

In this way, far from destroying objectivity, self-awareness creates both objectivity and subjectivity in the world, since self-
awareness is always subjective. Conversely, it is not objects that
disappear from the world when we close our eyes but an awareness of objects on the part of one of the objects in the world who
remains self-aware.

The experience of including the self in the world as a
self-aware person provides a basis for a further understanding,
namely, that other persons in the world possess self-awareness.
Once the self includes others as self-aware, then the self must

conclude reciprocally that the other persons are not only aware of the self but, in addition, are aware of the self as self-aware. Here, then, is the intersubjective dimension of ontology which creates the possibility of verification, community, and empathy.

Differences Between Models In Theology And In Science

This interweaving of epistemology and ontology, since it is a change in our theoretical framework, will cause us to see the world differently. We have said that such changes often are brought about by acts of metaphor justified by conviction resulting from limit-experience. In the next chapter we will test our theoretical framework to see if we do indeed see at least a part of the world differently than before. But for our final act of synthesis, there remains the task of reconsidering the theories characteristic of science and religion for the purpose of making explicit their similarities, their differences, and the sense in which each calls for, or mediates, the other. In order to do this, we move to a higher perspective than religion and science taken separately.

By and large we have seen that theories in science are expressions of a determinate understanding of specifiable data. Some theories in religion, such as Durkheim's sociological definition of religion or Marx's critique are also determinate understandings of specifiable data. Other theories in religion, such as Ramsey's disclosure theory, are determinate understandings of data less easily specified. Some few religious and theological theories make explicit, in addition, the limit-character of all human understanding. Tracy's theory of limit-concept is a good illustration of this latter kind of theory. It is on the basis of these few special theories which point beyond themselves that the following case can be made for a difference between religion and science. By means of a theory of limit, all understanding is itself understood to be partial in the sense that it points beyond the known-known and the known-unknown to the unknown-unknown (questions we can ask and answer, questions we can ask and can't answer, and questions we cannot even ask). This is not to say that theology posits "something" outside the theory. It is only to say that in

theology, some theories point beyond themselves to a totality residing within and at the same time transcending our ordinary everyday experience and understanding.

Does science have any such theory? Can we find evidence in
science of an explicit acknowledgement that determinate knowledge is limited? In Gödel's theorem we have an explicit denial
of the self-sufficiency presumed to be the case in scientific
theories. In 1931 Kurt Gödel, a mathematician, published a
short paper, "On Formally Undecidable Propositions of Principia
Mathematica and Related Systems," which according to Ernest
Nagel and James Newman, is now understood to be "one of the
most important advances in logic in modern times."[4] Gödel's
theorem states that there is no way to prove that any given mathematical system is closed. What Gödel's theorem does is to make
explicit the notion of limit—namely, that any mathematical
theory lacks the capacity for self-containment. We notice that
here the mode of making explicit is negative: there is no affirmation of limit. Nevertheless, Gödel's theorem is different from
most scientific theories, which, as we have said, express determinate understandings of specifiable data. We can see that scientific and religious theories differ, then, in the frequency with
which their theories point beyond themselves.

We are now prepared to formulate the sense in which science
and religion are interdependent. In its ability to give a theoretical status to our experience of limit and transcendence, theology
is in a sense "needed" by science. In its ability to give a theoretical status to our determinate understanding of specifiable data,
science is in a sense "needed" by theology. Since this is the case,
we can say that the worlds of religious and scientific meanings
mediate each other so that any understanding is impoverished
and any claim to truth less probable for lack of their interdependence. In the next chapter, we test the ways in which science
and religion each mediate the other by re-examining the concept
of mystery.

CHAPTER TEN

New Worlds—New Meanings

I‍F WE INSIST that knowledge (the model of science) and faith (the model of religion) be equated, new relations come into being as things to enlarge human understanding. Examples demonstrate the new curvature of our world of meanings, a distortion brought about by metaphoric process. The book ends with a reading of the familiar Genesis story, which is now seen as a narrative of the origin of knowledge-in-process.

NEW WORLDS

Epistemology as the science of knowing began in Greece over 2000 years ago. Today the Greek legacy is both a treasure and a hindrance. It forms the core of our common-sense understandings of the world which we know are too limited. Consider the law of the excluded middle—that what is, is; what is not, is not; nothing can both be and not be. The logic of infinitesimals, the paradoxes of Russell, the infinities of Cantor, the abstractions of modern quantum physics—all show that classical simplicity is no longer an adequate basis for thought. The concept of mutual embeddedness—that A is contained in B while at the same time B is contained in A—although contrary to the classical law of the excluded middle, can be found in the Christian eucharistic phrase " . . . that God may dwell in us and we in God." Only in classical terms, and in traditional common-sense intuitions, is it contradictory to think that religion as faith and revelation is contained in science and that science as systematic knowledge is contained in religion. In other words, science and religion are mutually embedded in much the same way humans and the world are mutually embedded: The world contains us even as we contain the world.

Gone also is the concept of eternal truth. Knowledge is seen as evolving, rather than as residing in dark corners waiting to be discovered. Process has replaced immutability, and knowledge-in-process has replaced knowledge as simple truth. Whereas traditional meanings of the terms contradiction and complexity tend to be uniformly negative or pejorative, today these terms have positive meanings as well. But common sense changes slowly, like the flow of rock, and only as a result of constant pressure. The human mind is fundamentally conservative, all too inclined to suffer those limitations it has rather than to open itself to others it knows not.

It follows that we cannot, with a stroke, create the global metaphor that will unite science as natural philosophy with religion. We can, however, by insisting that the two worlds are one, maintain the metaphoric pressure that may, in time, reform the naïve structure of simple worlds of meanings into complex structures rich with the freedom of new possibility.

DETECTING THE CURVATURE OF OUR WORLD

Up to this point our use of examples has been directed either to clarification of ideas by means of analogies or to elucidation of a particular concept by means of an examination of a specific case of its use. In this final chapter, examples will demonstrate the change in the topography of our world of meanings that has been brought about by our emphasis on epistemological process. We do not know how to do this from outside our own world of meanings, from a still higher viewpoint, so we must rely on our ability to study these effects from within. How might that be possible?

Consider a person who desires to travel in a large square on the surface of the earth. The person begins the journey at New York City and travels some 10,000 kilometers in a straight line (in any direction). To travel in a large square the person makes a right angle (90 degree) left turn at the end of the first leg and continues another 10,000 kilometers steering neither to the left nor to the right. The second leg of the journey completed, the traveler turns left again to begin the third leg of the great square. Continuing straight ahead on the third part of the journey, the traveler is surprised to find New York City at the end of the third leg of the great square journey instead of the fourth and only in facing this apparent contradiction comes to realize that the concept "square" has changed because that surface of the earth is curved. A kind of epistemological anxiety sweeps over us when our common-sense view of a world is shown to yield contradictions, but we must resist the inclination to cry out "nonsense." Instead we must develop an ability to engage the complexities that arise as contradiction transforms our world of meanings.

Bearing in mind the experience of the traveler, we will examine below certain aspects of the world that were established in chapter nine as aspects of both science and religion. If we insist that science and religion are the same world, we will be able to detect a "curvature" in our world of meanings, and we will no longer see these two intellectual fields as separate flat worlds.

RELATIVISTIC TIME

In chapter seven we described one aspect of relativistic time, the effect known as time dilation, which can be summarized in the statement: Moving clocks run slow. Another aspect, not mentioned earlier, is the destruction of the concept of universal simultaneity. Prior to the development of relativity at the beginning of the twentieth century, it was generally held that two events could take place at different locations and be understood to occur simultaneously. Einstein, however, showed that events appearing to be simultaneous to one observer will be seen as occurring at different times by another observer moving with respect to the first observer. Furthermore, since each observer's observations are equally valid, the idea of simultaneity loses significance and the possibility of absolute time must be abandoned.

The implications of the loss of validity of the concept of absolute time are far-reaching. Not only does time run more slowly for systems moving with large velocities, but anything that might travel at speeds greater than the speed of light would not be limited to one historical path through space. As Arthur Eddington observed, "Certainly matter cannot attain a greater speed [than the speed of light]; but there might be other things in nature which could. . . . It can scarcely be said to be a self-contradictory property to be in two places at the same time any more than . . . to be at two times in the same place."[1] Such observations challenge our common-sense view of the world. We struggle with our disbelief and if our disbelief can be overcome, we are prepared to believe in new possibilities.

Theologians have not been unaware of the implications of relativity theory. In the last chapter of his book, *Christian Hope* (1978), John Macquarrie, for example, urged his readers to

> take into account the understanding of time that has emerged in modern science, especially in relativity theory. . . . What is the significance of [Albert Einstein's relativity theory] for the [view] I was putting forward about the past being still present to God and alive in God, and about his power to heal and transform even the past? I think the significance is quite considerable, and should make it clear that to talk of God in such ways is not to indulge in a kind of theological science-fiction.[2]

In other words, Macquarrie holds that a common-sense understanding of the theory of relativity is not sufficient to inform contemporary theological understanding. As suggestive as novel scientific conceptions can be, however, they court the possibility of naïve interpretation and literalization. In the case of relativity theory, for example, it might be thought that our new understandings enlarge the realm of space time, whereas in fact our new understandings limit the realm of human influence even as they increase in complexity. In a relativistic space-time world, with presently known energy sources, the speed of matter is limited to that speed at which light travels, effectively limiting the distance a person can travel in a lifetime to about fifty light years—a paltry distance compared to the 100,000 light-year distance from one side of our galaxy to the other. Moreover, we realize that we cannot have any influence whatsoever on any activity that might be going on on the other side of our galaxy until the 100,000 years have elapsed that are required to send any signal from here to there. Accordingly, it would be mistaken to equate our new relativistic space time with the realm of God.

God remains, as stated in Anselm's ontological argument, "that than which nothing greater can be conceived."[3] We must resist any inclination to restrict God to one conceptual world, however vast any newly created world may seem to us at the time. Greek deities inhabited a concrete world outside time. They frequented mountains, coastal shores, and the seas of ancient Achaea but did not dwell explicitly in the t (time) of history. By contrast, the God of the Hebrew Testament was found not primarily in the x,y,z (space) of the Mesopotamian peninsula but existed in the flow of ordinary historical time. A concept of God in terms of the x,y,z,t of four-dimensional space time— however necessary a concept for contemporary theological intelligibility—is also space-time dependent.

More significant than any particular new concept may be the tendency of thought, its gradient and its direction. These are clues to the way thought moves and suggests the possibility of still newer concepts that may open up greater understanding. To see knowledge-in-process is to see not only how far we have come in the development of our understandings but also to realize how far we can expect to go in the future. This sense that we participate in an ongoing development can suggest extrapolations from our present states of knowledge to others which have not yet been grounded, even as relativity theory had not been grounded when Einstein asserted his confidence in its predictions.

More imaginative eschatologies consider the possibility that the moment of personal death is the transcendent moment, the new simultaneity, the one moment in which all humans are caught up with God or the Sacred—a vision of the millenium which could be used as the basis for a re-examination of religious beliefs of many traditions.

The statistical character of quantum theory is also suggestive. The probability that an atom of an unstable element will disintegrate is known to be independent of time. An atom of uranium 229, for example, has a fifty percent chance of disintegrating in the next hour. And if it survives the hour, its chance of disintegration in the succeeding hour continues to be fifty percent.

These data are based on theory and observation in nuclear physics, yet they seem counterintuitive when considered carefully. Suppose we were to take an alarm clock as a model of an unstable nucleus. The alarm clock is presumed to be set, and without looking to see what time it has been set to ring we ask the probability that it will ring in the next hour. Since we presume the clock will ring sometime in the next twelve hours, the probability of its ringing in the next hour is one-twelfth, the probability of its ringing in the following hour is one-eleventh and so on. The probability of the clock ringing increases with the passing of each hour until, in the twelfth hour, the probability has reached one—certainty. Suppose, now, that the clock does not ring in the twelfth hour. What can we conclude? We must conclude that the clock is not working, or that it was never set to ring in the first place. All of our thinking about the alarm clock is representative of the common-sense way we think about the probability of the occurrence of an expected event. The thinking is based on a mechanistic view of the world, a view that has been discredited by modern physics. We learn from science, from our unstable uranium nucleus, however, that the world is not fundamentally mechanical, that it is indeed possible for an event to have a probability of occurrence that does not change with time no matter how long we may wait. With this new understanding let us turn to a familiar eschatological passage in the Christian testament, attributed to the Christ:

> "I tell you solemnly, before this generation has passed away all these things will have taken place. . . . But as for the day or hour, nobody knows it, neither the angels of heaven, nor the Son; no one but the Father. Be on your guard, stay awake, because you will never know when the time will come."[4]

The literal interpretation of this passage by early Christians caused them to believe that the second coming and the fulfillment of all prophecy was an immanent event, each day that passed making it more likely to occur on the next day. After the passage of some 2000 years, many, today, are forced by a mechanistic model of the world to conclude that the event cannot reasonably be understood to occur in history. But now we see that a new understanding of the world, one brought about by an insistence that the world of nuclear physics is the same world as the world of history, permits us to interpret what this text refers to, not as figurative expression, based on a naïve common-sense probability, but as an event whose probability does not change with time, an event which may be immanent indefinitely.

It is clear that a common-sense view of time is deficient not only because it does not account for all the data but also in that it lacks the complexity that makes it possible to overwhelm the metaphoric contradiction. To "overwhelm" a metaphoric contradiction in a higher viewpoint is to provide a richness of possible interpretations that forestalls quick rejection of the distortions of our world of meanings until they have had the chance to be studied and evaluated in terms of their fruitfulness.

Complexity is to be found not only in the results of metaphoric process: it exists as well in the initial personal and private moments of metaphoric thought. Of special relevance to the process of coming-to-know is the statement of Einstein that he knew that his theory was right independently of any empirical observation that might be made in support of it: when asked, ". . . what if there had been no confirmation of his prediction, he countered, 'then I would have been sorry for the dear Lord—the theory *is* correct.'"[5] Such a posture, which seems audacious, must be based on a conviction that amounts to absolute fiat. It arises not from tests applied to the natural world but in some complex way out of the epistemological process itself. As an aid in perceiving and preserving this difficult-to-specify experience, some theoretical understanding is needed. For a systematic understanding of the psychological dimensions of the ontological flash, we turn to Abraham Maslow's account of his research into "peak-experience." We do this with some caution because of the disputed status of both psychology and epistemology, which we do not argue here. We turn to the psychological only to provide reasons for the affirmation (as well as the denial) of an "ontological flash" so that it can be understood as affecting the way humans are. In other words, it is a return, after our own exposition of the character of knowing, to the character of being.

ONTOLOGICAL FLASH AS PEAK-EXPERIENCE

A "peak-experience," according to Maslow, is a special moment of intense joy, reassurance, or creation, which suddenly
gives a vision of one's own unique being that, for a moment at
least, is at one with what is and will be. Descriptively, Maslow's
"peak-experience" already has some of the characteristics of the
"ontological flash": according to Maslow, a first-timeness, a "sense
of sheer unpreparedness and surprise" always accompanies a peak-
experience.[6]

His definition in hand, Maslow reported some interesting
points about his research. He began, he said, thinking that there
were some people who had such experiences and others (whom
he called "non-peakers") who didn't. But after he became more
skillful at asking questions to generate responses from those he
interviewed, he found that the percentage of subjects who reported peak-experiences grew higher and higher. He finally "fell
into the habit of expecting everyone to have peak-experiences
and of being rather surprised" if he ran across someone who could
report none at all. And so he began to use the word "non-
peaker" to describe "not the person who is unable to have peak-
experiences, but rather the person who is afraid of them, who
suppresses them, who denies them, who turns away from them,
or who 'forgets' them."[7] The non-peaker can be described in the
words of T.S. Eliot as one who "had the experience but missed
the meaning."[8]

Maslow speculated on the reasons why some people "renounce"
their peak-experiences. Any person "whose character structure
(or way of life) forces him to try to be completely rational or
materialistic or mechanistic tends to become a non-peaker."[9]
These circumstances lead the unreflective to regard their peak-
experiences as a loss of control, even a kind of insanity. Because
they are afraid of losing control, they reject peak-experiences.
Having organized their lives around the denying and controlling
of emotion, they obliterate such experiences from their memo-
ries. Maslow told of his interview with a politician who turned
away from a peak-experience, having classified it as some kind of
"peculiar but unimportant thing that had happened but that had

best be forgotten because this experience conflicted with her whole materialist philosophy of life."[10] For her, in other words, R_1 had to be subsumed into R_2.

Although Maslow by and large restricted his theory to "positive" experiences, he did compare peak-experience to a kind of death because of the disruption it brings about in our ordinary experience. The negative counterpart to Maslow's idea of peak-experience can be found in Karl Jaspers' concept of "boundary-situation."[11] A boundary-situation commonly includes guilt, anxiety, sickness, and the realization of death for oneself or another. This negative limit-experience (or nadir-experience) is an "ontological flash" in the sense that we have a sudden recognition that our best-laid plans, our fondest hopes and our prized accomplishments can suffer decline or distortion. When one experiences the time-dependency of existence, one has a sudden overwhelming vision of one's lack of independent being that, for a moment at least, is conjunctive with what is not and will not be. The understanding of both peak and nadir experiences rescues significant parts of common human experiences from oblivion, repression, but most especially from domestication—the sense that common human experience is routine, humdrum, and lacking in mystery.

These significant parts of common human experience are not commonplace even though they are common. The peak-experiences identified by Maslow and the boundary-situations of Jaspers are experiences similar to those which William James describes as religious. One of the salient features of James' *The Varieties of Religious Experience* is his effort to incorporate private experience (R_1 or S_1) into a science of religions. In spite of his cautious regard for theological speculation, James documented the cognitive persuasiveness of certain kinds of private experience as in the following provocative statements:

> You will in point of fact hardly find a religious leader of any kind in whose life there is no record of automatisms [inspiration which produces automatic, i.e., involuntary, utterances or actions]. . . . The whole array of Christian saints, . . . the Bernards, the Loyolas, the Luthers, the

Foxes, the Wesleys, had their visions, voices, rapt conditions, guiding impressions, and 'openings.' . . . Beliefs are
strengthened wherever automatisms corroborate them. In-
cursions from beyond the transmarginal region have a peculiar power to increase conviction. The inchoate sense of
presence is infinitely stronger than conception. . . .[12]

We notice that neither Maslow's nor James' account of private, personal experience is reductionist: Neither equates these
extraordinary occurrences with automatisms or physiological
manifestations—the increased heart rate, the flush of adrenalin,
the tingle of nerves—which may be coincident. Rather, Maslow,
James, and Jaspers make it possible for us to relate these special
experiences to other human experiences as experiences of things,
not merely of bodily sensations.

If we find intelligent persons resisting the conclusions of Einsteinian relativity or resisting an ontological flash on ostensible
psychological grounds, we should not be surprised to find the
conclusions embraced by others on the same grounds. Our own
argument, however, does not depend upon the psychological acceptance of one or another kind of experience, but on the ascer-
tained relationship between public and private experience and
knowledge. But as S_1 and R_1 become "known," do we not remove
the last remaining vestige of mystery from human existence?

MYSTERY AS KNOWLEDGE-IN-PROCESS

We must first of all put some restrictions on what we mean
by mystery. We will limit our meaning by observing what mystery is not. Mystery is not merely that which is unknown. The
unknown-unknown, strictly speaking, holds no mystery nor does
the entire realm of the known-known offer itself to us with any
aspect of mysteriousness. Therefore, for mystery we must look
into those cognitive realms which contain the known-unknown.
Moreover, mystery arises in response to question and resides in
the tension of inquiry, often in connection with an answer which
cannot be understood. To say that we see through the glass darkly
asserts that we do, to a limited extent at least, "see" and implies
further that we have directed our attention and are looking, that

we are motivated to look and we are moved by a need to know. If contradiction is fuel for knowledge-in-process, mystery is motivating force.

Some years ago a chemist and a physicist were engaged in a conversation regarding the purpose of science. The questions were philosophical, rather than sociological or technological, and were being considered from the point of view of natural philosophy with no particular regard for the utility of the fruits of scientific research. The conversation turned to the role of science as the means of answering questions about the natural world, and the chemist proposed the following hypothetical state of affairs:

Imagine that some power placed on this earth a machine that could answer any question put to it regarding the natural universe. Is it not the case that the existence of such a machine would signal the end of science? And does it not follow that the essential purpose of science is to answer any question we might pose about the natural universe?

The physicist was intensely dissatisfied with the state of affairs that was described by that proposition. Why was the presence of the omniscient machine so unsatisfactory? Surely it was not merely the sense of a desire to "do it for oneself" rather than have the machine do it, although that did seem to account for part of the discomfort. Then the proper response to the presence of such a machine suddenly became clear. One should fetch a screwdriver and disassemble the machine in order to come to know how it worked. One should respond but not to the possibility that the machine had eliminated the mystery in the world. For surely had that been the case there would be no more natural science. What one should respond to is the fact that the machine represented a new mystery in the world so that the mystery in the machine became itself the focus of science. To those who would quibble that one need only ask the machine how it worked, one could reply that the machine could not, *in toto*, understand its own workings as that would require more mechanism that the machine contained. Such additional mechanism the machine would not be able to explain because that would require more mechanism, etc. Complete self-explanation is never possible because it must be accomplished with respect, at least in part, to that which is not contained. Once again we hear an echo of Gödel's theorem.

Apart from the issue of the distinction between understanding and the ability to answer questions is the clear emergence of mystery as an essential component of science, at least from the point of view of natural philosophy. Quite contrary to some naïve understandings of scientific process, the true scientist is not dismayed encountering contradiction but rather welcomes the mystery and the challenge that contradiction can pose. In this sense mystery—the human approach to mystery in general, not particular mysteries—is an essential aspect of the pursuit of natural philosophy.

Whatever is said about mystery must not obscure its relation to our particular emphasis on knowledge-in-process: mystery in both religious and scientific thought must be understood in its dynamic aspects. Casual or liturgically routine reference made, for example, to "the holy mysteries," is not to be understood as implying something eternal which necessarily remains changeless. From the point of view of knowledge-in-process, that which is changeless is precluded because the human, in the process of coming-to-know, necessarily changes that which might otherwise be considered to be changeless.

And so how are we to understand that which is both mystery and change? We must have in mind something of the nature of a "quest" for mystery as a characterization of a religious mode of thought, not a quest for a "holy grail" as in the traditional example of a medieval pilgrimage, for that conjures up an object as a goal which is an already-out-there-now-real, but a movement toward a horizon that recedes as horizons always do, drawing us in contemporary pilgrimage, itself an achievement and not merely an attainment of some object-seen-as-goal.

Just as Maslow's peak-experiences imply that having a peak-experience does not preclude more such experiences subsequently, we do not exhaust awe and wonder and love by the experience of them. If a love is forever renewed, it is renewed not because it is forever new love but because it is forever a new person who loves. Experiences are renewed through changes in the individuals who have the experiences. And so it is with mystery. If in our quest for mystery we grow to find new mystery, we still understand that mystery or horizon or limit will never be exhausted.

The expectation that there is growth in mystery is not restricted to the field of religion. A case in point is the development of theories in science about the origin of the universe. Although the Big Bang theory of the origin of the universe was widely accepted, there seemed to be no possibility of dealing with the question of the origin of the Big Bang itself until Edward P. Tryon became convinced in 1973 of the possibility of the universe arising from nothing on the basis of quantum uncertainty principles. Tryon's description of his insight suggests that he experienced an ontological flash:

"The instant I saw the possibility I was so taken by it," he said. "I just felt, 'This is it!' That it was simple and beautiful and natural. That it was inevitable in the impersonal beauty of its logic."[13]

In a report on theories of the origin of the universe, including Tryon's theory, Alan MacRobert observed that in the history of such theories there has been one constant:

> We have gone from a single Earth to recognizing many planets, from one Sun to many suns, from one galaxy to many. In each case, those who advocated the larger view of things proved to be right. . . . We peer today as through a barely open door at a prospect of universes without end, great and small, familiar and incomprehensible, in numberless profusion.[14]

Here we have the mystery of limitlessness displaying the limitlessness of mystery.

And so, now, at the end of this story of the process of coming-to-know in science and religion, we read anew a text from the Book of Genesis, a text forever filled with mystery, but with mystery that changes because we change.

AN EPISTEMOLOGICAL ALLEGORY

The Serpent was the most subtle of all the wild beasts that Yahweh God had made. It asked the woman, "Did God really say you were not to eat from any of the trees in the garden?" The woman answered the serpent, "We may eat the fruit of the trees in the garden. But of the fruit of the tree in the middle of the garden God said, 'You must not eat it, nor touch it, under pain of death.'" Then the serpent said to the woman, "No! You will not die! God knows in fact that on the day you eat it your eyes will be opened and you will be like gods, knowing good and evil." The woman saw that the tree was good to eat and pleasing to the eye, and that it was desirable for the knowledge that it could give. So she took some of its fruit and ate it. She gave some also to her husband who was with her, and he ate it. Then the eyes of both of them were opened, and they realized that they were naked. So they sewed fig leaves together to make themselves loincloths.

The man and his wife heard the sound of Yahweh God walking in the garden in the cool of the day, and they hid from Yahweh God among the trees of the garden. But Yahweh God called to the man. "Where are you?" he asked. "I heard the sound of you in the garden," he replied. "I was afraid because I was naked, so I hid." "Who told you that you were naked?" he asked. "Have you been eating of the tree I forbade you to eat?" The man replied, "It was the woman you put with me; she gave me the fruit, and I ate it." Then Yahweh God asked the woman, "What is this you have done?" The woman replied, "The serpent tempted me and I ate."

Then Yahweh God said to the serpent, "Because you have done this,

"Be accursed beyond all cattle, all wild beasts. You shall crawl on your belly and eat dust every day of your life. I will make you enemies of each other: you and the woman, your offspring and her offspring. It will crush your head and you will strike its heel."

To the woman he said:

"I will multiply your pains in childbearing, you shall give birth to your children in pain. Your yearning shall be for your husband, yet he will lord it over you."

To the man he said, "Because you listened to the voice of your wife and ate from the tree of which I had forbidden you to eat,

"Accursed be the soil because of you. With suffering shall
you get your food from it every day of your life. It shall yield
you brambles and thistles, and you shall eat wild plants.
With sweat on your brow shall you eat your bread, until you
return to the soil, as you were taken from it. For dust you are
and to dust you shall return."

The man named his wife "Eve" because she was the mother of
all those who live. Yahweh God made clothes out of skins for the
man and his wife, and they put them on. Then Yahweh God
said, "See, the man has become like one of us, with his knowledge of good and evil. He must not be allowed to stretch his
hand out next and pick from the tree of life also, and eat some
and live for ever." So Yahweh God expelled him from the garden
of Eden, to till the soil from which he had been taken. He banished the man, and in front of the garden of Eden he posted the
cherubs and the flame of a flashing sword to guard the way to the
tree of life.[15]

Traditional interpretations of this allegory suggest that it expresses the origin of evil, an evil associated with human sexual-
ity and expressed with almost the same force as the apocryphal
fall of Lucifer (Rev. 12:7-9). Contemporary interpretations, attempting to overcome the sexual prejudice, treat the man as pas-
sively accepting the fruit and the woman as "active, intelligent,
and decisive."[16] But it is also possible to understand the first act
of Adam and Eve as told in the story of Genesis, not as a sexual
act, but as an epistemological act. The first thing they did together was to yield to the temptation of the serpent (curiosity)
and eat the fruit because Eve saw that "it was desirable for
the knowledge that it could give." The immediate effect of this
was that "their eyes were opened" (the first ontological flash)
and they "realized that they were naked" (they became self-
conscious).

And so the first man and the first woman were banished from
paradise. Why? Because they "sinned" (disobeyed God)? No, we
choose to think rather that they were expelled because otherwise
they might have eaten of the Tree of Life which would have re-

stored their immortality and made them truly gods. To be God is not just to be immortal, that earlier state into which the man and woman were born, but to both know and be immortal. In effect then the choice was between knowing and living forever, and they chose to know. The serpent was wrong. God did not lie. Both Adam and Eve died.

For us, as epistemologists, the story is also an allegory explaining the origin of the human need to know as the birth of knowledge-in-process, a story that begins but never ends.

Notes

CHAPTER ONE

1. Ludwig Wittgenstein, *Tractatus Logico-Philosophicus* (London and Henley: Routledge & Kegen Paul, 1961), #1.1, p. 5.
2. Norwood Russell Hanson, *Patterns of Discovery* (London: Cambridge University Press, 1972), esp. p. 24.
3. Thomas S. Kuhn, *The Structure of Scientific Revolutions* (Chicago and London: The University of Chicago Press, Second Edition, 1970).
4. The uncritical use of Paul Tillich's notion of "ultimate concern" is an example of what we call uncritical ecumenism: the supposition that every person can be said to have an ultimate concern which is understood in itself to be religious. Tillich himself is reported as quipping, "Give me fifteen minutes with a person, and I'll tell you who that person's God is" (Riverside Lectures, 1960).
5. Langdon Gilkey, *Religion and the Scientific Future* (Harper & Row, 1970), pp. 69, 79, 89, 135. It is unfortunate that the use of what has come to be recognized as sexist language, for example, the use of "man" for "human," dominates the literature on science and religion. We have quoted exactly, however, rather than alter the text of quotations when this fault occurs. We presume that the authors themselves would have avoided the problem if they were writing today.
6. Harold Schilling, *The New Consciousness in Science and Religion* (Philadelphia: Pilgrim Press, 1973), p. 100.
7. Ian Barbour, *Myths, Models, and Paradigms* (New York: Harper & Row, 1974), pp. 4–5.
8. Earl MacCormac, *Metaphor and Myth in Science and Religion* (Durham: Duke University Press, 1976).
9. Alfred North Whitehead, *Science and the Modern World* (New York: Macmillan, 1925), p. 162.

CHAPTER TWO

1. Hanson, p. 6ff.
2. Ibid.
3. For an elaboration of Bernard Lonergan's distinction between bodies and things, see below in chapter two and note 16.

4. See Don Ihde, *Technics and Praxis* (Boston: Reidel, 1979), p. 6ff. See also Michael Polanyi, *Personal Knowledge* (New York: Harper Torchbook, 1964), pp. 55–56: "Think how a blind man feels his way by the use of a stick, which involves transposing the shocks transmitted to his hand and the muscles holding the stick into an awareness of the things touched by the point of the stick."
5. F.C. Müller-Lyer, "Optische Urteilstauschungen," *Arch. Physiol. Suppl*, Bd. 2, 263–70 (1899).
6. Hanson, p. 23.
7. Jean Bodin, as quoted in T.S. Kuhn, *The Copernican Revolution* (New York: Vintage Books, 1957), p. 190.
8. William James, *The Varieties of Religious Experience* (New York: New American Library, 1958), p. 326.
9. Ibid., p. 29.
10. Ibid., p. 32. In James' words, "Immediate luminousness, in short, philosophical reasonableness, and moral helpfulness are the only available criteria" (our omission of italics).
11. "Consciousness-raising" as an experience is particularly apt for calling attention to those aspects of experience which clearly exceed the sense-perception model. See also David Tracy, *A Blessed Rage for Order* (New York: Seabury, 1975), pp. 64–66.
12. Luke 24:13–35.
13. Bernard Lonergan, *Method in Theology* (New York: Herder & Herder, 1972), pp. 3–25.
14. "37 Who Saw Murder Didn't Call the Police," *New York Times*, 27 March, 1964, p. 1, col. 4. See also "What Kind of People are We?" (editorial), *New York Times*, 25 March, 1964, p. 18, col. 2.
15. Bernard Lonergan, *Grace and Freedom* (New York: Darton, Longman & Todd, 1971), esp. pp. 41–61.
16. In this chapter, we distinguish mediated understanding from direct experience and immediate experience in both science and religion. This parallel distinction does not imply a necessary equivalence between direct experience and immediate experience. By direct experience we mean a non-instrumentally mediated experience of an object—the object being understood either in relation to the self (in which case the object is understood as a body) or in relation to other objects (in which case the object is understood as a thing). By immediate experience, we mean an experience of an object in relation to the self (in which case the object is understood only as a body).

17. Bernard Lonergan, *Collection I*, ed. by F. E. Crowe (Herder & Herder, 1967), p. 253.

18. Ibid.

19. Lonergan, *Insight: A Study of Human Understanding* (London: Longmans, 1957), chapter eight, especially pp. 245–258.

20. Ibid.

CHAPTER THREE

1. For an elaboration of first and second naïveté, see chapter four below.

2. Antony Flew, *Thinking Straight* (Buffalo: Prometheus Books, 1977), p. 31.

3. Barry M. Casper and Richard J. Noer, *Revolutions in Physics* (New York: Norton, 1972), pp. 4–5.

4. Lewis Fry Richardson, quoted in Benoit B. Mandelbrot, *Fractals, Form, Chance, and Dimension* (San Francisco: W. H. Freeman & Co., 1977), p. 30.

5. This example is derived from a similar analysis given in Mandelbrot, p. 27ff.

6. Whitehead, pp. 51–54.

7. Ibid., p. 54.

8. To interpret a text requires some prior understanding of the text. The first interpretation incorporates the previous understanding, and all subsequent interpretations incorporate those interpretations which precede them. . . . We are in a hermeneutical circle.

9. Ian Ramsey, *Religion and Science: Conflict and Synthesis* (London: SPCK, 1964): "God is bound to abdicate, indeed we might say to disappear altogether, in the face of scientific progress" (p. 5).

10. Lonergan, *Method in Theology*, pp. xii, 3–25.

11. Karl Rahner, *Foundations of Christian Faith* (New York: Seabury, 1978), pp. 15–16.

12. Ibid., p. 16.

13. Ibid.

14. Ibid. Rahner cites as an example theologians who, he says, "are always in danger of talking about . . . God and human with an arsenal of religious and theological concepts . . . and perhaps not have really understood . . . what they are really talking about."

15. Ibid., p. 18.

16. Ibid., p. 20.

17. Ibid.

18. Ibid.
19. Ibid., p. 23.
20. Ibid., p. 22.
21. Reinhold Seeberg, *The History of Doctrines* (Grand Rapids: Baker Book House, 1966), pp. 201–218.
22. Ibid., pp. 267–272.
23. Monika Hellwig, "Christian Theology and the Convenant of Israel," *Journal of Ecumenical Studies* 7 (Winter, 1970), 49. See also Tarsicius van Bavel, "Chalcedon: Then and Now," in *Jesus, Son of God?*, ed. by Edward Schillebeeckx and Johannes-Baptist Metz, *Concilium* 153, pp. 55–62.
24. Rahner, p. 20.
25. Tracy, *A Blessed Rage for Order*, pp. 97–100.
26. Arthur Koestler, *The Sleepwalkers* (New York: Grosset & Dunlap, 1959).

CHAPTER FOUR

1. Quotations are from a poetry reading by Robert Bly at Hobart and William Smith Colleges in 1975.
2. MacCormac, pp. 102–34, ad passim.
3. David Tracy, *The Achievement of Bernard Lonergan* (New York: Herder & Herder, 1970), pp. 1–21.
4. MacCormac, p. 106.
5. Ibid., p. 103.
6. Ibid.
7. Ricoeur, *The Symbolism of Evil* (Boston: Beacon Press, 1960), pp. 350–62.
8. We have borrowed Ricoeur's terminology of first and second naïveté but have departed somewhat from his meaning. By first naïveté, Ricoeur refers to the immediacy of belief by a non-critical consciousness. By second naïveté, he means both that the critical consciousness cannot return to an immediacy of belief and that belief is mediated in terms of new understanding.
9. Gerald Holton, *Thematic Origins of Scientific Thought* (Cambridge: Harvard, 1973), pp. 11–44.
10. Ibid., pp. 18, 23.
11. Ibid., p. 17.
12. See Abraham Maslow, *Religions, Values, and Peak-experiences* (New York: Viking Press, 1970); I. T. Ramsey, *Religion & Science: Conflict*

& *Synthesis* (London: SPCK, 1964), especially pp. 42–43; Tracy, *Blessed Rage for Order*, especially chapter five, pp. 91–118.

13. Max Planck, *Scientific Autobiography and Other Papers*, (New York: Philosophical Library, 1949), pp. 33–34.
14. Emanuel Velikovski, *Worlds in Collision* (New York: Macmillan, 1950).
15. Bart J. Bok and Lawrence E. Jerome, *Objections to Astrology* (Buffalo: Prometheus Books, 1975), pp. 9–17.
16. Ibid., p. 10.
17. Holton, p. 18.
18. The unfortunate parallel in this instance extends to contemporary religion as well. In January, 1975, eighteen theologians of different denominations met in Hartford, Connecticut, and issued a document entitled "An Appeal for Theological Affirmation" which, as it was reported later in *The Christian Century*, "raised the charge of heresy against liberal theological view." Some theologians who were originally invited to sign the document refused, not because they necessarily disagreed with the propositions but because they objected to the form of the declaration. "I do not approve of anathemas," Langdon Gilkey said of his refusal to sign in "Anathemas and Orthodoxy," *The Christian Century*, 94 (November 9, 1977), 1026–1029.
19. Holton, p. 26.
20. In Malcolm Diamond, *Contemporary Philosophy of Religion* (New York: McGraw-Hill, 1974), pp. 135–136.
21. John B. Cobb, Jr. *The Structure of Christian Existence* (Philadelphia: Westminster, 1967), pp. 119–120.

CHAPTER FIVE

1. Holton, p. 64.
2. Ibid., p. 62.

CHAPTER SIX

1. Holton, p. 19ff.
2. MacCormac, p. 100–101.
3. Plato, *Gorgias*, in *The Collected Dialogues of Plato*, Bollinger Series, LXXI (Princeton: Princeton University Press, 1964).

4. Aristotle, *The Rhetoric* and *The Poetics*, ed. by Friedrich Solmsen (New York: The Modern Library, 1954).
5. Quintilian, *De Institutione Oratoria Libri Duodecim*, VIII (Leipzig, 1798, 1834).
6. Pierre Fontanier, *Les Figures du discourse*, as quoted by Paul Ricoeur, *La Métaphore vive* (Paris: Editions du Seuil, 1975), pp. 63–86.
7. Georg Wilhelm Friedrich Hegel, *Vorlesungen über die Aesthetic*, Vol. II. pp. 141–44.
8. Ibid.
9. I. A. Richards, *The Philosophy of Rhetoric* (London: Oxford University Press, 1936), pp. 89–112.
10. Susanne Langer, *Philosophy in a New Key* (Cambridge: Harvard U. Press, 1942), p. 141.
11. Philip Wheelwright, *The Burning Fountain: A Study in the Language of Symbolism* (Bloomington: Indiana University Press, 1954) Revised Edition, 1968, esp. pp. 61–62, 112–17.
12. Max Black, *Models and Metaphors: Studies in Language and Philosophy* (Ithaca: Cornell University Press, 1962), pp. 25–47.
13. Mary Hesse, *Models and Analogies in Science* (Notre Dame Press, 1970), pp. 158–59.
14. Ricoeur, *La métaphore vive*, pp. 252, 380. The English translation is *The Rule of Metaphor: An Interdisciplinary Study* (Toronto: University of Toronto, 1977).
15. Ibid., p. 319.
16. Ricoeur, *Interpretation Theory: Discourse and the Surplus of Meaning* (Fort Worth: Texas Christian U., 1976).
17. Ricoeur, "The Metaphorical Process as Cognition, Imagination, and Feeling," *Critical Inquiry*, 5 (Autumn, 1978), 143–59.
18. Samuel Levin, *The Semantics of Metaphor* (Baltimore: Johns Hopkins University Press, 1977).
19. For contemporary theological studies which explicitly raise the issue of metaphorical language, see the following: F. W. Dillistone, *Christianity and Symbolism* (London: William Collins Pub., 1955); Amos Wilder, *Early Christian Rhetoric* (Cambridge: Cambridge University Press, 1964); Robert W. Funk, *Language, Hermeneutic and Word of God* (New York: Harper and Row, 1966); Frederick Ferré, "Metaphors, Models and Religion," *Soundings*, 51 (Fall, 1968), 327–45; David Burrell, *Analogy and Philosophical Language* (New Haven: Yale University Press, 1973); Eleanor McLaughlin, "'Christ my Mother': Feminine Naming and Metaphors in Medi-

eval Spirituality," *St. Luke's Journal of Theology*, 18 (#4), 1975; Nicholas Lash, "'Son of God': Reflections on a Metaphor," *Jesus, Son of God?* (Edinburgh/New York: T. & T. Clark Ltd./The Seabury Press, 1982); Sallie McFague, *Metaphorical Theology: Models of God in Religious Language* (Philadelphia: Fortress Press, 1982). Several other theologians can be read as having taken for granted the importance of metaphor for theology. See, for example, Reinhold Niebuhr's comment that Biblical symbols are to be taken "seriously but not literally," *The Nature and Destiny of Man*, Vol. 2 (New York: Charles Scribner's Sons, 1955), p. 50.

20. David Tracy, "Metaphor and Religion: The Test Case of Christian Texts," *Critical Inquiry*, 5 (Autumn, 1978), 91–106.

21. McFague, see especially chapter five, "God the Father: Model or Idol?" pp. 145–92. See also p. 15 for her definition of metaphor.

CHAPTER SEVEN

1. Ernest Bloch, *Man on His Own* (New York: Herder and Herder, 1971), p. 60.
2. David Tracy, "Holy Spirit as Philosophical Problem," *Commonweal*, 8 (November, 1968), 208.
3. Friedrich Schleiermacher, *The Christian Faith* (Edinburgh: T. & T. Clark, 1928).
4. John B. Noss, *Man's Religions*, Fifth ed., (New York/London: Macmillan Collier, 1974), pp. 40–44.
5. Ibid., p. 129–31.
6. Corinthians 15:8.
7. Ibid., 15:23.
8. Handel's *Messiah*.
9. MacCormac, p. 102.
10. This definition of religion is based on Van A. Harvey, *The Historian and the Believer: The Morality of Historical Knowledge and Christian Belief* (New York: Macmillan, 1966).
11. Wilfred Cantwell Smith, *Towards a World Theology: Faith and the Comparative Religions* (Philadelphia: Westminster, 1981), pp. 64–74.
12. George Lakoff and Mark Johnson, *Metaphors We Live By* (Philadelphia: Westminster, 1981), pp. 64–74.
13. Holton, p. 168.
14. Quoted in ibid., p. 170.
15. Ibid., p. 32.

CHAPTER EIGHT

1. Martin J. Klein, *Physics Today* 31 (May, 1978), 69.
2. Bertrand Russell, *The Scientific Outlook*, quoted in Casper and Noer, p. 3.
3. Casper and Noer, p. 29.
4. Ibid.
5. Ibid.
6. Harold McCord, "Ontology," in *Maps: Poems Toward an Iconography of the West* (Santa Cruz: Kayak Books, 1971).
7. Martin Heidegger, *Being and Time* (New York: Harper & Row, 1962), p. 2.
8. Ibid., p. 27: "This entity which each of us is himself and which includes inquiring as one of the possibilities of its Being, we shall denote by the term 'Dasein.'"
9. *Hegel's Phenomenology of Spirit*, trans. by A. V. Miller (Oxford: Clarendon Place, 1977), p. 14: "The spiritual alone is the actual; it is the essence, or that which has being in itself; it is that which *relates itself to itself* and is *determinate*, it is *other-being* and being-for-self, and in this determinateness, or in its self-externality, abides within itself; in other words, it is *in and for itself*."
10. Charles Taylor, *Hegel* (Cambridge: Cambridge University Press, 1975), p. 237.
11. *Hegel's Phenomenology of Spirit*, p. 9.
12. *The Thirteen Principal Upanishads*, trans. by R. E. Hume (London: Oxford University Press, 1934), Chand. 6.12, p. 247.
13. Noss, p. 101.
14. Matthew 13:10–17.
15. Tracy, *A Blessed Rage for Order*, pp. 204–36.
16. Wallace Stevens, "Notes Toward a Supreme Fiction," in *The Collected Poems of Wallace Stevens* (New York: Alfred A. Knopf, 1969), pp. 404.

CHAPTER NINE

1. Wallace Stevens, "Asides on an Oboe," p. 250–51.
2. Wittgenstein, *Tractatus*, #2.01.
3. Ibid., #2.031.
4. Ernest Nagel and James R. Newman, *Gödel's Proof* (New York: New York University Press, 1958).

CHAPTER TEN

1. Sir Arthur Eddington, *Space, Time and Gravitation* (New York: Harper Torchbooks, 1959), p. 60.
2. John Macquarrie, *Christian Hope* (New York: Seabury, 1978), p. 125.
3. In John E. Smith, *Philosophy of Religion* (London: The Macmillan Company, 1965), p. 29.
4. Mark 13:30–32.
5. As quoted in Holton, pp. 236–37.
6. Maslow, p. xv.
7. Ibid., p. 22.
8. T. S. Eliot, *Four Quartets* (New York: Harcourt, Brace & World, 1943), p. 39.
9. Maslow, p. 22.
10. Ibid., p. 23.
11. Karl Jaspers, *Philosophie*, Vol. 2 (Berlin: J. Springer, 1956, pp. 117ff.
12. James, pp. 467–68.
13. Edward P. Tryon, as quoted in Alan MacRobert, "Beyond the Big Bang," *Sky and Telescope*, 65 (March, 1983), 211–12. See also Edward P. Tryon, "Is the Universe a Vacuum Fluctuation?" *Nature*, 246 (December 14, 1973), 396–97.
14. MacRobert, 213.
15. Genesis 3:1–24.
16. Jean Higgins, "Anastasius Sinaita and the Superiority of the Woman," *Journal of Biblical Literature*, 97:2, 253–56.

Select Bibliography

AMONG THE WORKS consulted in the preparation of this book the following are especially recommended for further study. It should be borne in mind, however, that most of the authors have not distinguished analogy and metaphor as we have. The terms are often used interchangeably, and examples termed metaphors would in some cases be considered by us to be analogies.

Barbour, Ian G. *Myths, Models, and Paradigms: A Comparative Study in Science & Religion*. New York: Harper & Row, 1974. An attempt to redress the loss of credibility with respect to the meaningfulness of religious language.

Black, Max. *Models and Metaphors: Studies in Language and Philosophy*. Ithaca: Cornell University Press, 1962. A work that renewed scholarly interest in the subject of metaphor.

Casper, Barry M. and Richard J. Noer. *Revolutions in Physics*. New York: Norton, 1972. A detailed survey of the historical discontinuities in both classical and modern physics, including suggested readings and questions.

Embler, Weller. *Metaphor and Meaning*. DeLand, FA: Everett/ Edwards, 1966. One of the first efforts to relate metaphor to thought and not merely to language.

Gilkey, Langdon. *Religion and the Scientific Future*. New York: Harper and Row, 1970. An attempt to bridge the gap between modern technological society and religious thought.

Hanson, Norwood Russell. *Patterns of Discovery*. Cambridge: Cambridge University Press, 1972. A detailed explication of the development of understanding in science from a philosophical and linguistic perspective.

Hesse, Mary. *Models and Analogies in Science*. Notre Dame: Notre Dame Press, 1970. The pioneering work that demonstrated that the development of ideas in science followed a process that paralleled the idea of analogy in language.

Holton, Gerald. *Thematic Origins of Scientific Thought*. Cambridge: Harvard, 1973. A theoretical structure for relating the private thoughts and actions of scientists to scientific work as presented in the scientific literature. Special attention is given to the historical and personal experiences that attended the development of the Theory of Relativity.

Hooykaas, R. *Religion and the Rise of Modern Science*. Grand Rapids: William B. Eerdmans Pub. Co., 1972. A study of the religious legacy of modern and and contemporary science.

James, William. *The Varieties of Religious Experience*. New York: Longmans Green and Co., 1902. The classic work on the relationship of psychology to religion.

Johnson, Mark, ed. *Philosophical Perspectives on Metaphor*. Minneapolis: University of Minnesota Press, 1981. A collection of fifteen essays on metaphor from I. A. Richards to Lakoff and Johnson, together with an annotated bibliography of lesser known sources.

Jones, James W. *The Texture of Knowledge: An Essay on Religion and Science*. Washington: University Press of America, 1981. A short but sensitive explication of the relations between religion and science, also from an epistemological point of view.

Jones, Roger S. *Physics As Metaphor*. Minneapolis: University of Minnesota Press, 1982. Metaphors and analogies are mixed together in this often amusing if iconoclastic description of scientific method by a physicist who does not take physics too seriously.

Kuhn, Thomas S. *The Structure of Scientific Revolutions*. Chicago and London: The University of Chicago Press, Second edition, 1970. The original work in which Kuhn introduced the concept of "paradigm-shift" for discontinuous parts of the history of science.

Lakoff, George and Mark Johnson. *Metaphors We Live By*. Chicago and London: The University of Chicago Press, 1980.

Sprightly detective work on the multiple ways metaphors shape everyday meanings.

Leatherdale, W. H. *The Role of Analogy, Model and Metaphor in Science.* New York: American Elsevier Publishing Co., Inc., 1974. A book that provides an exhaustive set of references to works published prior to 1970, though little distinction is made between metaphor and simile.

Lonergan, Bernard J. F. *Insight: A Study of Human Understanding.* Westminster: Christian Classics, 1957. A careful "little" book of 785 pages which is one of the best philosophical studies of "knowing."

————. *Method in Theology.* New York: Herder and Herder, 1972. See especially the chapters on "method" and "meaning."

MacCormac, Earl R. *Metaphor and Myth in Science and Religion.* Durham: Duke University Press, 1976. An argument that the linguistic methods in science and religion are the same.

McFague, Sallie. *Metaphorical Theology: Models of God in Religious Language.* Philadelphia: Fortress Press, 1982. A proposal to reconceive the field of theology as metaphorical and to reformulate specific concepts in that field in liberationist terms.

Macquarrie, John. *Christian Hope.* New York: Seabury, 1978. A study which suggests insightful conjunctions between contemporary science and traditional theology.

Maslow, Abraham. *Religions, Values, and Peak-experiences.* New York: Viking Press, 1970. An attempt to construct a psychological theory of experience which differentiates between everyday experience and trans-sensory experience.

Ortony, Andrew, ed. *Metaphor and Thought.* Cambridge: Cambridge University Press, 1979. A collection of papers from a conference on metaphor held in 1977. Of special interest is the section on metaphor and education in which metaphor emerges as significant to pedagogy in a way that is parallel to our use of metaphor in epistemology.

Pannenberg, Wolfhart. *Theology and the Philosophy of Science.* Philadelphia: Westminster Press, 1976. An argument by a theologian that theology is appropriately understood as a science.

Peacocke, A. R. *Science and the Christian Experiment*. London: Oxford University Press, 1971. A scientist's description of science and religion as "experienced human activities."

Polanyi, Michael. *Personal Knowledge: Towards a Post-Critical Philosophy*. New York and Evanston: Harper & Row, 1958. An account of science that frees it from positivism. See especially the chapter on "intellectual passions."

Ramsey, I. T. *Religion & Science: Conflict & Synthesis*. London: SPCK, 1964. See especially the notion of "disclosure-situation."

Richards, I. A. *The Philosophy of Rhetoric*. London: Oxford University Press, 1936. Source of the interaction theories of metaphor.

Ricoeur, Paul. *Interpretation Theory: Discourse and the Surplus of Meaning*. Fort Worth: Texas Christian University Press, 1976. A collection of four essays on written and spoken language, metaphor and symbol, explanation and understanding.

————. *The Rule of Metaphor: An Interdisciplinary Study*. Toronto: University of Toronto Press, 1977. A historical-critical study of metaphor, including a discussion of the incommensurability between metaphor and philosophical discourse.

Rogers, Robert. *Metaphor: A Psychoanalytic View*. Berkeley: University of California Press, 1978. A study of the psychological aspects of the metaphoric process, which locates metaphor not only in a verbal context but in the "mind, heart, bowels, glands, and other organs of the engaged and introjecting reader."

Romanyshyn, Robert D. *Psychological Life: From Science to Metaphor*. Austin: University of Texas Press, 1982. A critique of the use of psychological terms and meanings and an attempt to construct a metaphoric understanding of the discipline.

Sacks, Sheldon, ed. *On Metaphor*. Chicago and London: The University of Chicago Press, 1978. A collection of papers from a conference on metaphor held in 1978.

Schilling, Harold K. *The New Consciousness in Science and Religion*. Philadelphia: A Pilgrim Press Book, 1973. A scientist's description of the differences between modern and post-

modern science and the effects of the latter on the present-day
"transformation of human consciousness."

Schlesinger, George. *Religion and Scientific Method*. Dordrecht
and Boston: D. Reidel Publishing Co., 1977. An application
of scientific method to the study of theism, as related to the
issue of free will and the problem of evil.

Toulmin, Stephen. *Human Understanding*. Vol. 1. Princeton:
Princeton University Press, 1972. A study of the forms and
disciplines of understanding.

Tracy, David. *The Analogical Imagination: Christian Theology and
the Culture of Pluralism*. New York: Crossroad, 1981. A comprehensive study of theology as public, pluralistic and peren-
nial. See especially the chapters on the "classic" and the "religious classic."

————. *Blessed Rage for Order: The New Pluralism in Theology*.
New York: The Seabury Press, 1975. An argument that the
religious interpretation of human experience is both meaningful and true. See especially the chapters on "theological models" and the concept of "limit" in chapter five.

Whitehead, Alfred North. *Science and the Modern World*. New
York: The Macmillan Co., 1925. The classic critique of historical differences between science and religion since the seventeenth century and an argument for their reconciliation as
necessary for human understanding.

Acknowledgments

The poem, "Ontology" from *Maps: Poems Toward an Iconography of the West*, copyright 1971 by Kayak Books, is reprinted by permission of the author, Howard McCord.

The illustration, "Still Life and Street" by M.C. Escher (jacket art and figure 6.5) from the book *The World of M.C. Escher*, copyright 1971 by Harry N. Abrams, is reprinted by permission of M.C. Escher Heirs, c/o J.W. Vermeulen, Prilly, CH.

We are indebted to a number of persons who read all or part of early versions of this manuscript and who made helpful comments, especially Professors Paul Ricoeur, John E. Thiesmeyer, and David Tracy.

Index of Names

209

Index of Subjects

213